Robert B. Reich

Beyond Outrage

Robert B. Reich is Chancellor's Professor of Public Policy at the Richard and Rhoda Goldman School of Public Policy at the University of California, Berkeley. He has served in three national administrations, most recently as secretary of labor under President Bill Clinton, and he served as an adviser to President-elect Barack Obama. He has written twelve books, including *The Work of Nations* (which has been translated into twenty-two languages), *Supercapitalism,* and the best sellers *The Next American Frontier, The Future of Success, Locked in the Cabinet,* and, most recently, *Aftershock: The Next Economy and America's Future.* His articles have appeared in *The New Yorker, The Atlantic, The New York Times,* the *Financial Times, The Washington Post,* and *The Wall Street Journal.* He is co-founding editor of *The American Prospect* magazine and chairman of Common Cause. His biweekly commentaries on public radio's *Marketplace* are heard by nearly five million people. In 2003, Reich was awarded the prestigious Václav Havel Foundation Prize for pioneering work in economic and social thought. In 2008, *Time* magazine named him one of the ten most successful cabinet secretaries of the twentieth century, and *The Wall Street Journal* named him one of the nation's ten most influential business thought-leaders.

www.robertreich.org

ALSO BY ROBERT B. REICH

Aftershock

Supercapitalism

Reason

I'll Be Short

The Future of Success

Locked in the Cabinet

The Work of Nations

The Resurgent Liberal

Tales of a New America

The Next American Frontier

AS EDITOR

The Power of Public Ideas

AS CO-AUTHOR, WITH JOHN D. DONAHUE

New Deals: The Chrysler Revival and the American System

Beyond Outrage

Beyond Outrage

What Has Gone Wrong with
Our Economy and Our Democracy,
and How to Fix It

Robert B. Reich

Illustrated by the Author

VINTAGE BOOKS

A Division of Random House, Inc.

New York

FIRST VINTAGE BOOKS EDITION, SEPTEMBER 2012

Copyright © 2012 by Robert B. Reich

All rights reserved. Published in the United States by
Vintage Books, a division of Random House, Inc., New York,
and in Canada by Random House of Canada Limited, Toronto.
Originally published in somewhat different form as an e-short
by Alfred A. Knopf, a division of Random House, Inc., New York.

Vintage and colophon are registered trademarks
of Random House, Inc.

Library of Congress Cataloging-in-Publication Data
Reich, Robert B.
Beyond outrage : what has gone wrong with our economy and our
democracy, and how to fix it / Robert B. Reich.
p. cm.
ISBN 978-0-345-80437-2 (alk. paper)
1. United States—Economic policy—Citizen participation.
2. Right and left (Political science). 3. Conservatism—United States.
4. Democracy—United States. I. Title.
HC106.84.R453 2012
330.973—dc23
2012025077

Book design by Christopher M. Zucker

www.vintagebooks.com

Printed in the United States of America
10 9 8 7 6 5 4 3 2 1

To the Occupiers, and all others committed to taking back
our economy and our democracy

Contents

Introduction

I've written this book to give you the big picture of why and how our economy and our democracy are becoming rigged against average working people, what must be done, and what you can do about it. I've called it *Beyond Outrage* for a very specific reason. Your outrage is understandable. Moral outrage is the prerequisite of social change. But you also need to move beyond outrage and take action. The regressive forces seeking to move our nation backward must not be allowed to triumph.

I have been involved in public life, off and on, for more than forty years. I've served under three presidents. When not in office, I've done my share of organizing and rabble-rousing, along with teaching, speaking, and writing about what I know and what I believe. I have never been as concerned as I am now about the future of our democracy, the corrupting effects of big money in our politics, the stridency and demagoguery of the regressive right, and the accumulation of wealth and power at the very top. We are perilously close to losing an economy and a democracy that are meant to work for everyone and to replacing them with an economy and a government that will exist mainly for a few wealthy and powerful people.

This book is meant to help you focus on what needs to be done and how you can contribute, and to encourage you not to feel bound by what you think is politically possible this year or next. You need to understand why the stakes are so high and why your participation—now and in the future—is so important. I've tried to array concepts and arguments in a way that you'll find helpful. All the facts I've cited are from government reports unless otherwise indicated.

In my experience, nothing good happens in Washington unless good people outside Washington become mobilized, organized, and energized to make it happen. Nothing worth changing in America will actually change unless you and others like you are committed to achieving that change.

Connecting the Dots

The first thing you need to do is connect the dots and understand how many troubling but seemingly unrelated things are interwoven. The challenge we face is systemic. The fundamentals of our economy are out of whack, which has distorted our democracy, and these distortions, in turn, are making it harder to fix the economic fundamentals. Later in the book we'll examine several of these dots in detail, but now I'd like you to see the big picture.

The first dot: For three decades almost all the gains from economic growth have gone to the top. In the 1960s and 1970s, the wealthiest 1 percent of Americans got 9–10 percent of our total income. By 2007, just before the Great Recession, that share had more than doubled, to 23.5 percent. Over the same period the wealthiest one-tenth of 1 percent *tripled* its share. We haven't experienced this degree of concentrated wealth since the Gilded Age of the late nineteenth century. The 400 richest Americans now have more wealth than the entire bottom half of earners—150 million Americans—put together. Meanwhile, over the last three decades the wages of the typical worker have stagnated, averaging only about $280 more a year than thirty years ago, adjusted for inflation. That's less than a 1 percent gain over more than a third of a century. Since 2001, the median wage has actually dropped.

This connects to . . .

The second dot: The Great Recession was followed by an anemic recovery. Because so much income and wealth have gone to the top, America's vast middle class no longer has the purchasing power to keep the economy going—not, at least, without going deeper and deeper into debt. But debt bubbles burst. The burst of 2008 ushered in a terrible recession—the worst economic calamity to hit this country since the Great Depression of the 1930s—as middle-class consumers had to sharply reduce their spending and as businesses, faced with declining sales, had to lay off millions. We bottomed out, but the so-called recovery has been one of the most anemic on record. That's because the middle class still lacks the purchasing power to keep the economy going and can no longer rely on borrowing.

While at the same time . . .

The third dot: Political power flows to the top. As income and wealth have risen to the top, so has political clout. Obviously, not everyone who's rich is intentionally corrupting our democracy. For those so inclined, however, the process is subtle and lethal. In order to be elected or reelected, politicians rely greatly on advertising, whose costs have risen as campaign spending escalates. They find the money where more and more of the money is located—with CEOs and other top executives of big corporations and with traders and fund managers on Wall Street. A Supreme Court dominated by conservative jurists has opened the floodgates to unlimited amounts of money flowing into political campaigns. The wealth of the super-rich also works its way into politics through the corporations they run or own, which employ legions of lobbyists and public relations experts. And their wealth buys direct access to elected officials in informal dinners, rounds of golf, overnight stays in the Lincoln Bedroom, and fancy boondoggles.

Which connects to . . .

The fourth dot: Corporations and the very rich get to pay lower taxes, receive more corporate welfare, and are bound by fewer regulations. Money paid to politicians doesn't enrich them directly; that would be illegal. Rather, it makes politicians dependent on their patrons in order to be reelected. So when top corporate executives or Wall Street traders and managers want something from politicians they have backed, those politicians are likely to respond positively. What these patrons want most are lower taxes for themselves and their businesses. They also want subsidies, bailouts, government contracts, loan guarantees, and other forms of corporate welfare, and fewer regulations. The tax cuts enacted in 2001 and 2003— and extended for two years in 2010—in 2011 saved the richest 1.4 million taxpayers (the top 1 percent) more money than the rest of America's 140,890,000 taxpayers received in total income.

Leading to . . .

The fifth dot: Government budgets are squeezed. With so much of the nation's income and wealth at the top, tax rates on top earners and corporations dropping, and most workers' wages stalling or declining, tax revenues at all levels of government have fallen precipitously. This has led to a major squeeze on public budgets at all levels of government. The result has been deteriorating schools, less college aid, crowded and pockmarked highways, unsafe bridges, antiquated public transportation, unkempt parks, fewer police officers, fewer social workers, and the decline of almost everything else the broader public relies on.

Which connects to . . .

The sixth dot: Average Americans are competing with one another for slices of a shrinking pie. There is now more intense competition for a dwindling number of jobs, a smaller share of total income, and ever more limited public services. Native-born Americans are threatened by new immigrants; private sector workers are resentful of public employees; non-unionized workers are threatened by the unionized; middle-class Americans are competing with the poor. Rather than feel that we're all in it together, we increasingly have the sense that each of us is on his or her own.

Which leads, finally, to . . .

The seventh dot: A meaner and more cynical politics prevails. Because of all these occurrences, our politics has become nastier, more polarized, and increasingly paralyzed. Compromise is more difficult. Elections are more venomous, political advertising increasingly negative. Angry voters are more willing to support candidates who vilify their opponents and find easy scapegoats. Talking heads have become shouting heads. Many Americans have grown cynical about our collective ability to solve our problems. And that cynicism has become a self-fulfilling prophecy, as nothing gets solved.

Connect these dots and you understand why we've come to where we are. We're in a vicious cycle. Our economy and our democracy depend on it being reversed. The well-being of your children and grandchildren requires it.

In Part One, I describe how the game is becoming rigged against average working people and in favor of wealthy plutocrats and large corporations. In Part Two, I explain the rise of the regressive right, a movement designed not to conserve what we have but to take America backward toward the social Darwinist ideas that prevailed in the late nineteenth century. In Part Three, I suggest what you can do to reverse this perilous course.

Part One

The Rigged Game

I receive many e-mails from people who have read my columns or who have seen me in the media. Some e-mails are very friendly; others are hostile. But almost all share a common feature. The writers believe the game is rigged. Here's a composite of several I've received from people who describe themselves as Tea Partiers:

> Mr. Reich,
>
> I saw you on television just now. You want to raise taxes on the rich so there's more money for education and infrastructure. You're a stupid ass. When taxes go up, it's people like me who end up paying more because the rich always find ways to avoid paying. If you think the money will go to helping average Americans, you're even dumber. Government is run by Wall Street traders, the CEOs of big corporations, and military contractors. They'll get the benefits. Where

were you when my taxpayer dollars were used to bail out fuck-
ing Wall Street? The answer is less government, not more. Do
me a favor and shut up.

I don't recall so many people, regardless of political party
or ideology, expressing so much outrage and cynicism about
our economic and political system.

The presidential candidate Mitt Romney said free enterprise is on trial. He's right, but it's not on trial in the way
he assumed. The attack on it is not coming from the left.
It's coming from the grass roots of America—right, left, and
center. And it's been triggered by an overwhelming consen-
sus that Wall Street, big corporations, and the very wealthy
have rigged it to their benefit. Increasingly, the rewards have
gone to the top, while the risks have been borne by middle-
and lower-income people. At the same time, the very wealthy
are getting a greater share of total income than they did at
any point in the last eighty years. Their tax rates are lower
than they've been in a generation. Republicans want us to
believe that the central issue is the size of government, but
the real issue is whom government is for. Public institutions
are deteriorating. We're saddled by the most anemic recovery from the worst economy since World War II, while the
basic bargain linking pay to productivity continues to come
apart.

FREE ENTERPRISE ON TRIAL

In the late 1980s, I noticed a troubling trend. A larger and
larger share of the nation's income and wealth was going to
the very top—not just the top 1 percent, but the top of the

top 1 percent—while other Americans were dividing up a shrinking share. I wrote up my findings, and my tentative explanation for this trend, in a book called *The Work of Nations*. Bill Clinton read the book, and after he was elected president, he asked me to be his secretary of labor. He told me he was committed to reversing the trend, and he called for more investment in education, training, infrastructure, and health care in order to make the bottom half of our population more productive. Clinton and his administration worked hard, but we were never able to implement his full agenda. The economic recovery of the middle and late 1990s was strong enough to generate twenty-two million new jobs and raise almost everyone's wages, but it did not reverse the long-term trend. The share of total income and wealth claimed by the top continued to grow, as did the political clout that accompanies such concentration. Most Americans remained unaware.

But now the nation is becoming aware. President Obama has made it one of the defining issues of his reelection campaign. The nonpartisan Congressional Budget Office has issued a major report on the widening disparities. The issue has become front-page news. For the first time since the 1930s, a broad cross section of the American public is talking about the concentration of income, wealth, and political power at the top.

Score a big one for the Occupiers. Regardless of whether you sympathize with the so-called Occupier movement that began spreading across America in the fall of 2011, or whether you believe it will become a growing political force in America, it has had a profound effect on the national conversation.

Even more startling is the change in public opinion. Not

since the 1930s has a majority of Americans called for redistribution of income or wealth. But according to a *New York Times*/CBS News poll, an astounding 66 percent of Americans say the nation's wealth should be more evenly distributed. A similar majority believes the rich should pay more in taxes. According to a *Wall Street Journal*/NBC News poll, a majority of people who describe themselves as Republicans believe taxes should be increased on the rich.

I used to be called a class warrior for even raising the subject of widening inequality. Now it seems most Americans have become class warriors. Or at least class *worriers*. And many blame Republicans for stacking the deck in favor of the rich. In that *New York Times*/CBS News poll, 69 percent of respondents said Republican policies favor the rich (28 percent said the same of President Obama's policies).

The old view was that anyone could make it in America with enough guts and gumption. We believed in the self-made man (or, more recently, woman) who rose from rags to riches: inventors and entrepreneurs born into poverty, like Benjamin Franklin; generations of young men from humble beginnings who grew up to become president, like Abraham Lincoln. We loved the novellas of Horatio Alger and their more modern equivalents—stories that proved the American dream was open to anyone who worked hard. In that old view, which was a kind of national morality play, being rich was proof of hard work, and lack of money was proof of indolence or worse.   .

A profound change has come over America. Guts, gumption, and hard work don't seem to pay off as they once did—or at least as they did in our national morality play. Instead, the game seems rigged in favor of people who are already rich and powerful—as well as their children. Instead of lion-

Widening inequality
loss of democracy
Citizen's United
Casino capitalism
regressives' political power
Wall Street back to its old tricks
tax cuts for rich
we're losing good jobs
loss of public services
bailouts for rich and for Wall Street but home owners under water

with apologies to Edvard Munch.

izing the rich, we're beginning to suspect they gained their wealth by ripping us off.

As recently as a decade ago the prevailing view was also that great wealth trickled downward—that the rich made investments in jobs and growth that benefited all of us. So even if we doubted that we ourselves would be wealthy, we assumed we'd still benefit from the fortunes made by a few. But that view, too, has lost its sheen. Americans see that nothing has trickled down. The rich have become far richer over the last three decades, but the rest of us haven't benefited. In fact, median incomes are dropping.

Wall Street moguls are doing better than ever—after having been bailed out by taxpayers. But the rest of us are doing worse. CEOs are hauling in more than three hundred times the pay of average workers (up from forty times the pay only three decades ago). But average workers have been losing their jobs and wages. The ratio of corporate profits to wages is higher than it's been since before the Great Depression. The chairman of Merck took home $17.9 million in 2010, as Merck laid off sixteen thousand workers and announced layoffs of twenty-eight thousand more. The CEO of Bank of America raked in $10 million, while the bank announced it was firing thirty thousand employees.

Even though the rate of unemployment has begun to fall, jobs still remain scarce, and the pay of the bottom 90 percent continues to drop, adjusted for inflation. But CEO pay is still rising through the stratosphere. Among the CEOs who took in more than $50 million in 2011 were Qualcomm's Paul Jacobs ($50.6 million), JCPenney's Ron Johnson ($51.5 million), Starbucks's Howard Schultz ($68.8 million), Tyco International's Ed Breen ($68.9 million), and Apple's Tim Cook ($378 million). The titans of Wall Street are doing even better.

The super-rich are not investing in jobs and growth. They're putting their bonanza into U.S. Treasury bills or investing it in Brazil or South Asia or anywhere else it can reap the highest return. The American economy is in trouble because so much income and wealth have been going to the top that the rest of us no longer have the purchasing power to keep the economy going. I'll get into this in greater detail shortly.

Some apologists for this extraordinary accumulation of income and wealth at the top attribute it to "risk taking" by courageous entrepreneurs. Mitt Romney defines free enterprise as achieving success through "risk taking." The president of the Chamber of Commerce, Tom Donohue, explains that "this economy is about risk. If you don't take risk, you can't have success." But in fact the higher you go in today's economy, the easier it is to make a pile of money without taking any personal financial risk. The lower you go, the bigger the risks and the smaller the rewards.

Partners in private-equity firms like Romney's Bain Capital don't risk their own money. They invest other people's money and take 2 percent of it as their annual fee for managing the money regardless of how successful they are. They then pocket 20 percent of any upside gains. Partners like Romney pay taxes on only 15 percent of what they make—a lower rate than that paid by many middle-class Americans— because of a loophole that treats this income as capital gains. The ostensible reason capital gains are taxed at a much lower rate than ordinary income is to reward investors for risking their money, but private-equity managers usually don't risk a dime.

In fact, rather than taking any real risks, they get government to subsidize them. Having piled the companies they purchase with debt, private-equity managers then typically issue "special dividends" that repay the original investors. Interest payments on that mountain of debt are tax deductible. In effect, government subsidizes them for using debt instead of incurring any real risk with equity. If the companies are subsequently forced into bankruptcy because they can't manage payments on all this debt, they dump their pension obligations on the Pension Benefit Guaranty Corporation (PBGC), a federal agency, which picks up the tab. If the PBGC can't meet the payments, taxpayers are left holding the bag.

It's another variation on Wall Street's playbook of maximizing personal gain and minimizing personal risk. If you screw up royally, you can still walk away like royalty. Taxpayers will bail you out. Personal responsibility is completely foreign to the highest echelons of the Street. Citigroup's stock fell 44 percent in 2011, but its CEO, Vikram Pandit, got at least $5.45 million on top of a retention bonus of $16.7 million. The stock of JPMorgan Chase fell 20 percent, but its CEO, Jamie Dimon, was awarded a package worth $22.9 million.

The higher you go in corporate America as a whole, the less of a relationship there is between risk and reward. Executives whose pay is linked to the value of their firm's shares get a free ride when the stock market as a whole rises, even if they didn't lift a finger. On the other hand, to protect their wallets against any risk that their firm's share price might fall, they can place countervailing bets in derivatives markets. This sort of hedging helped the head of AIG, Hank Greenberg, collect $250 million in 2008, when AIG collapsed.

Other CEOs are guaranteed huge compensation regardless of how their companies do. Robert Iger's arrangement as head of the Disney Company netted him $52.8 million in 2011 and guarantees him at least $30 million a year more through 2015—regardless of company performance. The swankiest golf courses of America are festooned with former CEOs who have almost sunk their companies but been handsomely rewarded. Gilbert Amelio headed Apple for a disastrous seventeen months while the firm lost nearly $2 billion, but he walked away with $9.2 million anyway. William D. McGuire was forced to resign as CEO of United-Health over a stock-options scandal but left with a pay package worth $286 million.

It doesn't even matter how long you're at the helm.

Thomas E. Freston lasted just nine months as CEO of Viacom before being terminated with an exit package of $101 million. Scott Thompson lasted only four months as CEO of Yahoo!, but that was long enough for him to pocket $7 million. His predecessor, Carol Bartz, lasted twenty months and left with an exit package of $10.4 million.

You can push your company to the brink and still make a fortune. Robert Rossiter, the former CEO of Lear, landed his company in bankruptcy, which wiped out his shareholders along with twenty thousand jobs, but he walked away from the wreckage with a $5.4 million bonus. In early 2012, *The Wall Street Journal* looked into the pay of executives at twenty-one of the largest companies that had recently gone through bankruptcy. The median compensation of those CEOs was $8.7 million—not much less than the $9.1 million median compensation of all CEOs of big companies. The reason CEOs get giant pay packages for lousy performance is that they stack their boards of directors' compensation committees with cronies who make sure they do.

Even if you commit fraud, your personal financial risk is minimal. Starting in 2009, the Securities and Exchange Commission (SEC) filed twenty-five cases against mortgage originators and securities firms. A few are still being litigated, but most have been settled. They generated almost $2 billion in penalties and other forms of monetary relief, according to the SEC. But almost none of this money came out of the pockets of CEOs or other company officials; it came out of the companies—or, more accurately, their shareholders. In the one instance in which company executives appear to have been penalized directly—a case brought against three former top officials of New Century Financial, a brazenly fraudulent lender that subsequently collapsed—

the penalties were tiny compared with how much the executives pocketed. New Century's CEO had to disgorge $542,000 of his ill-gotten gains, but he took home more than $2.9 million in "incentive" pay in the two years before the company tanked.

Yet as economic risks are vanishing at the top and the rewards keep growing, the risks, as I said, are rising dramatically on almost everyone below, and the rewards keep shrinking. Full-time workers who put in decades with a company can now find themselves without a job overnight—with no parachute, no help finding another job, and no health insurance. More than 20 percent of the American workforce is now "contingent"—temporary workers, contractors, independent consultants—with no security at all.

Most families face the mounting risk of receiving giant hospital bills yet having no way to pay them. Fewer and fewer large and medium-sized companies offer their workers full health-care coverage—74 percent did in 1980; under 10 percent do today. As a result, health insurance premiums, co-payments, and deductibles are soaring.

Most people also face the increasing risk of not having enough to retire on. Three decades ago more than 80 percent of large and medium-sized firms gave their workers "defined benefit" pensions that guaranteed a fixed amount of money every month after they retired. Now it's fewer than 10 percent. Instead, the employers offer "defined contribution" plans, where the risk is on the workers. When the stock market plunges, as it did in 2008, 401(k) plans plunge along with it. Meanwhile, people at the top are socking away tens of millions for their retirements while paying little or no taxes—in effect, enjoying a huge government subsidy. By 2011, Mitt Romney's IRA was worth between $20 million and $100 million, including Bain Capital holdings in off-shore havens like the Cayman Islands.

Romney is right: free enterprise is on trial. But he's wrong about the question at issue in that trial. It's not whether America will continue to reward risk taking. It's whether an economic system can survive when those at the top get giant rewards no matter how badly they screw up while the rest of us get screwed no matter how hard we work.

GOVERNMENT'S SIZE ISN'T THE
REAL ISSUE—IT'S WHOM GOVERNMENT IS FOR

Americans have never much liked government. After all, the nation was conceived in a revolution against government. But the surge of cynicism engulfing the country isn't about government's size. The cynicism comes from a growing perception that government isn't working for average people. It's seen as working for big business, Wall Street, and the very rich—who, in effect, have bought it. In a recent Pew Research Center poll, 77 percent of respondents said too much power is in the hands of a few rich people and corporations. That view is understandable.

Wall Street got bailed out by American taxpayers, but by 2012 one out of every five homeowners with a mortgage was still underwater, caught in the tsunami caused by the Street's excesses. The federal bailout wasn't conditioned on the banks helping these homeowners, and after the bailout direct federal help to homeowners was meager. The government's settlement of claims against the banks was tiny compared with how much homeowners lost. As a result, millions of people have lost their homes or simply walked away from homes whose mortgage payments they could no longer afford.

Homeowners couldn't use bankruptcy to reorganize their mortgage loans, because the banks have engineered the bankruptcy laws to prohibit this. Young people can't use bankruptcy to reorganize their student loans either, because the banks have barred it. But big businesses now routinely use bankruptcy to renege on contracts with their workers. American Airlines entered bankruptcy in 2012 and promptly announced plans to fire thirteen thousand workers—16 percent of its workforce—while cutting back the health benefits of current employees. It had intended to terminate its underfunded pension plans, threatening the largest pension default in U.S. history—much of whose cost would be borne by taxpayers if the Pension Benefit Guaranty Corporation took them over. (The airline subsequently backed down, freezing but not terminating the pensions.)

By 2012, long after the economic collapse, average consumers and small businesses were still hurting, but corporations large enough to finance fleets of Washington lobbyists were raking it in. Big agribusiness continues to claim hundreds of billions of dollars in price supports and ethanol subsidies, paid for by American consumers and taxpayers. Big Pharma gets extended patent protection that drives up everyone's drug prices, plus the protection of a federal law making it a crime for consumers to buy the same drugs at lower prices from Canada. Big oil gets its own federal tax subsidy, paid for by taxpayers.

Not a day goes by without Republicans decrying the federal budget deficit. But the biggest single driver of the yawning deficit is big money's corruption of Washington. One of the federal budget's largest and fastest-growing programs is

Medicare, whose costs would be far lower if Medicare could use its bargaining leverage to get drug companies to reduce their prices. It hasn't happened, because the lobbyists for Big Pharma won't allow it. Medicare's administrative costs are only 3 percent, far below the 30 percent average administrative costs of private insurers. So it would seem logical to tame rising health-care costs for all Americans by allowing any family to opt in. That was the idea behind the "public option." But health insurers' representatives stopped it in its tracks.

The other big budgetary expense is national defense. America spends more on our military than do China, Russia, Britain, France, Japan, and Germany combined. The "basic" defense budget (the annual cost of paying troops and buying planes, ships, and tanks—not including the costs of actually fighting wars) keeps growing. With the withdrawal of troops from Afghanistan, the cost of fighting wars is projected to drop, but the base budget is scheduled to rise. It's already about 25 percent higher than it was a decade ago, adjusted for inflation. One big reason for that is the near impossibility of terminating large defense contracts. Defense contractors have cultivated sponsors on Capitol Hill and located their plants and facilities in politically important congressional districts. Lockheed Martin, Bechtel, Raytheon, and others have made spending on national defense into America's biggest jobs program.

So we keep spending billions on Cold War weapons systems like nuclear attack submarines, aircraft carriers, and manned combat fighters that pump up the bottom lines of defense contractors but have nothing to do with twenty-first-century combat. In 2012 the Pentagon said it wanted to buy fewer F-35 Joint Strike Fighter planes than had been planned—the single-engine fighter has been plagued by cost overruns and technical glitches—but the contractors and their friends on Capitol Hill vowed to fight the decision.

Meanwhile, government regulators who are supposed to protect the public too often protect the profits of big companies that supply regulators with good-paying jobs when they retire from government and that give key members of Congress fat campaign contributions when they run for reelection. Consider the safety of nuclear reactors. General Electric marketed the Mark 1 boiling-water reactors that were used in Japan's Fukushima Daiichi plant as cheaper to build than other reactors because they used a smaller and less expensive containment structure. The same design is used in twenty-three American nuclear reactors at sixteen plants. But are Mark 1 reactors safe? In the mid-1980s, Harold Denton, then an official with the Nuclear Regulatory Commission (NRC), said Mark 1 reactors had a 90 percent probability of bursting should the fuel rods overheat and melt in an accident. Japan tragically experienced that probability a quarter century later. But so far, the NRC has done nothing except examine the issue.

The national commission appointed to investigate BP's giant oil spill in the Gulf of Mexico concluded that BP failed to adequately supervise Halliburton's work on installing the well. This was the case even though BP knew Halliburton lacked experience in testing cement to prevent blowouts and hadn't performed adequately before on a similar job. Neither company bothered to spend the money to ensure sufficient testing. It was much the same story at Massey Energy, owner of the West Virginia coal mine where an explosion in April 2010 killed twenty-nine miners. Massey wouldn't spend the money needed to ensure its mines were safe. It had a history of safety violations but did nothing in response other than fighting them or refusing to pay the fines.

No company can be expected to build a nuclear reactor, an oil well, a coal mine, or anything else that's 100 percent safe under all circumstances; the costs would be prohibitive. It's unreasonable to expect corporations to totally guard against small chances of every potential accident. Inevitably, there's a trade-off. Reasonable precaution means spending as much on safety as the probability of a particular disaster occurring, multiplied by its likely harm to human beings and the environment if it does occur.

But profit-making corporations have every incentive to underestimate these probabilities and lowball the likely harms. This is why it's necessary to have government regulators and why regulators need enough resources to enforce the rules. And it's why moves in Congress to cut the budgets of agencies charged with protecting public safety are so wrongheaded. One such proposal would reduce funding for the tsunami warning system. Another would ban the Environmental Protection Agency from regulating air pollution, including cancer-causing contaminants.

It's also why regulators must be independent of the industries they regulate. A revolving door between a regulatory agency and an industry makes officials reluctant to bite the hands that will feed them. In Japan, it's common for regulators to retire to better-paying jobs in the industries they were supposed to have regulated, a practice known there as *amakudari*. The United States, sadly, is no different. Remember the Department of the Interior's Minerals Management Service, whose officials were supposed to regulate offshore drilling? Many of them now occupy cushy jobs in oil companies. Remember the financial regulators who were supposed to oversee Wall Street before the Street almost melted down, and others who were supposed to oversee the taxpayer-funded bailout of the Street afterward? Many of them are now collecting fat paychecks on the Street.

Protecting the public doesn't have to be wildly expensive. But regulators and regulatory agencies have to be independent and smart. The public cannot be safe as long as big corporations—including GE, BP, Halliburton, Massey, and the biggest Wall Street banks—are allowed in effect to bribe legislators and entice regulators. Here again, the game is increasingly rigged, and most Americans are paying the price.

"Big government" isn't the problem. The problem is the big money that's taking over government. Government is doing fewer of the things most of us want it to do—providing good public schools and affordable access to college, improving our roads and bridges and water systems, maintaining safety nets to catch people who fall, and protecting the public from dangers—and more of the things big corporations, Wall Street, and wealthy plutocrats want it to do.

Some conservatives argue, like my composite e-mail correspondent, that we wouldn't have to worry about big money taking over government if we had a smaller government to begin with. They say the reason big money is swamping our democracy is that a large government attracts big money. When I debated with Congressman Paul Ryan on ABC-TV's *This Week,* he said that "if the power and money are going to be here in Washington, that's where the influence is going to go . . . that's where the powerful are going to go to influence it." Ryan has it upside down. A smaller government that's still dominated by money would continue to do the bidding of Wall Street, the pharmaceutical industry, oil companies, big agribusiness, big insurance, military contractors, and rich individuals. It just wouldn't do anything else.

THE BIG-MONEY TAKEOVER

Millionaires and billionaires aren't making huge donations to politicians out of generosity. Corporations aren't spending hundreds of millions of dollars on lobbyists and political campaigns because they love America. These expenditures are considered investments, and the individuals and corporations that make them expect a good return. The reason that the oil industry gets $2.5 billion a year in special tax subsidies, for example, has nothing to do with the public's interest and everything to do with the $150 million a year big oil spends on political campaigns. A $2.5 billion return on $150 million isn't bad, especially considering added benefits that come in the form of votes to expand oil drilling rights and pipelines.

The 2012 presidential race would be the priciest ever, costing an estimated $2 billion or more. "It is far worse than it has ever been," said the Republican senator John McCain. And an overwhelming share of the money would come from a handful of wealthy individuals and large corporations. All restraints on spending were off now that the Supreme Court had determined that money is speech—it can't be limited— and corporations are people under the First Amendment.

So-called super PACs would become the private slush funds of billionaires seeking political influence and a means of fulfilling narcissistic appetites for sheer power. The Texas billionaire Harold Simmons, for instance, would pour at least $12 million into the anti-Obama super PAC "American Crossroads" and even more into super PACs dedicated to getting Mitt Romney elected president. It seems doubtful Simmons's main motivation was the public good. He had built a West Texas dump for radioactive wastes bigger than a thousand football fields, which he could fill only with the aid of a friendly administration in Washington along with pliant environmental regulators.

The same mix of pecuniary and egoistic motives lay behind the super PAC contributions of other billionaires. The casino magnate Sheldon Adelson would pour at least $60 million into the 2012 election, seeking in part to protect foreign tax shelters worth billions. Super PAC spending via the Wyoming mutual-fund honcho Foster Friess was said to have powered Rick Santorum's upset win in the Iowa caucuses, which in turn kept Santorum going for months. Not since the Gilded Age had a handful of super-rich individuals so easily used their fortunes to fuel the presidential ambitions of a few people so radically out of the mainstream of American politics.

Meanwhile, nonprofit political fronts like Crossroads GPS, founded by the Republican political guru Karl Rove, gathered hundreds of millions of dollars from big corporations and wealthy individuals like the billionaire oil and petrochemical moguls David and Charles Koch and poured the money like poison into the veins of American politics. The U.S. Chamber of Commerce, under the control of Tom Donohue, became a repository for corporations wanting to influence politics without their customers or even shareholders knowing. Under Internal Revenue Service regulations, such nonprofit "social welfare organizations" were not required to disclose the names of those who contributed to

them. How many billionaires and big corporations does it take to buy the presidency and Congress? We would soon find out—although we would not know many of their names.

In May 2012, *Politico* revealed that Republican super PACs and other outside groups shaped by a network of conservatives—led by Karl Rove, the Koch brothers, and Tom Donohue—planned to spend about $1 billion on the 2012 election for the White House and control of Congress. Koch-related organizations also planned to spend $400 million ahead of the 2012 elections, including county-by-county operations in key states. All this outside spending would be in addition to traditional party fund-raising: the Romney campaign and the Republican National Committee intended to raise $800 million. If all of them—the outside groups and the Republican campaigns—hit their targets, they would outspend Democrats two to one. (President Obama's super PAC hoped to spend $100 million. Organized labor aimed for $200 million to $300 million.)

Never before in the history of our republic would so few spend so much to influence the votes of so many. Just the spending linked to the Koch brothers' network exceeded the $370 million John McCain raised for his entire presidential election in 2008. And the $1 billion that outside groups intended to raise from the super-rich and from corporations for the 2012 elections surpassed the $750 million Barack Obama collected in his 2008 campaign.

Yet when real people without money assemble to express their dissatisfaction with all this, they're told the First Amendment doesn't apply. Instead, they're clubbed, pepper sprayed, thrown out of public parks, and evicted from public spaces. Across America, public officials forced Occupiers out of places that had once been open to peaceful assembly. Even in universities—where free speech is supposed to be sacrosanct—students have been met with clubs and pepper spray.

The threat to America is not coming from peaceful demonstrators. And it's not coming from a government that's too large. It's coming from unprecedented amounts of money now inundating our democracy, mostly from big corporations and a handful of the super-rich. And it is happening precisely at a time when an almost unprecedented share of the nation's income and wealth is accumulating at the top.

We cannot tolerate inordinate wealth for the few along with unbridled money in politics. As the great jurist and Supreme Court justice Louis Brandeis once said, "We may have democracy or we may have great wealth concentrated in the hands of a few, but we can't have both."

The Great Switch of the Super-Rich

One of the major returns to the rich from their political investments has been lower taxes. Forty years ago, wealthy Americans helped finance the U.S. government far more than now through their tax payments. Today wealthy Americans help finance the government mainly by lending it money. While foreigners own most of our national debt, over 40 percent is owned by Americans—mostly the very wealthy.

This great switch by the super-rich—from primarily paying the government taxes to now lending the government money—has gone almost unnoticed. But it's critical for understanding the predicament we're now in. And for getting out of it.

From World War II until 1981 the top marginal income tax rate never fell below 70 percent. Under President Dwight Eisenhower, a Republican whom no one ever accused of being a socialist, the top rate was 91 percent. Even after all deductions and credits, Americans with incomes of over $1 million (in today's dollars) paid a top marginal rate, on average, of 52 percent. As recently as the late 1980s, the top tax rate on capital gains was 35 percent.

But as income and wealth have accumulated at the top, so has the political power to reduce taxes. The Bush tax cuts of 2001 and 2003, which were extended for two years in December 2010, capped top rates at 35 percent, their lowest level in more than half a century, and reduced capital gains taxes to 15 percent. In the half century spanning 1958 to 2008, the average effective tax rate of the richest 1 percent of Americans—including all deductions and tax credits—dropped from 51 percent to 26 percent. During the same period the typical middle-class taxpayer went from paying 15 percent of income in taxes to 16 percent.

In 2011, according to the Internal Revenue Service, the four hundred richest Americans paid an average of 17 percent of their income in taxes. That's lower than the tax rates of many middle-class Americans, as I've already said. Mitt Romney paid less than 14 percent on income in excess of $20 million, in both 2010 and 2011. That's because so much of the income of the super-rich is classified as capital gains, which, at 15 percent, creates a loophole large enough for the super-rich to drive their Ferraris through. Well-heeled tax lawyers and accountants are kept busy year-round figuring out how to make the earnings of their clients look like capital gains. Congress still hasn't closed the "carried interest" loophole that allows mutual-fund and private-equity managers to treat their incomes as capital gains.

Great wealth creates opportunities for ever greater tax loopholes. In 2010, eighteen thousand American households earning more than half a million dollars paid no income taxes at all. The estate tax (which affects only the top 2 percent) has also been slashed. As recently as 2000 it was 55 percent and kicked in after $1 million. Today it's 35 percent and kicks in at $5 million.

At the same time, the share of government revenue coming from corporations has been dropping—due in no small part to squadrons of corporate lawyers and lobbyists finding and creating ways to cut their companies' tax bills. American companies are booking higher profits than ever, but corporate tax receipts as a share of profits are at their lowest level in at least forty years. According to the Congressional Budget Office, corporate federal taxes paid in 2011 dropped to 12.1 percent of profits earned from activities within the

United States—a sharp decline from the 25.6 percent on average that companies paid from 1987 to 2008. The nation's biggest corporations, like GE, find ways to pay no federal taxes at all. Congress has quietly cooperated, creating tax breaks that allow companies to write off investments or shelter their earnings abroad.

The only major tax increases in recent years have fallen on the rest of America. Middle- and lower-income Americans are shelling out larger portions of their sinking incomes in payroll taxes, sales taxes, and property taxes than they did thirty years ago. The Social Security payroll tax continues to climb as a share of total government tax revenues. Yet the payroll tax is regressive, applying only to yearly income under $110,100 (the ceiling in 2012). That means it takes a far bigger bite out of the pay of the middle class and the working poor than out of the rich. Sales taxes at the state and local levels are soaring, along with property taxes and tolls on highways, bridges, and tunnels. These also take bigger percentage bites out of the incomes of average Americans than they do out of those of the rich.

What are the super-rich and big corporations doing with all their savings? They've put significant sums into Treasury bills—essentially loans to the U.S. government—which have proven to be good and safe investments, particularly during these last few tumultuous years. Hence the great switch of the super-rich. Maybe I'm old-fashioned, but it seems to me people at the top, who have never had it so good, should sacrifice a bit more. That way the rest of us—who are struggling harder than Americans have struggled since the 1930s— won't have to sacrifice quite as much.

Some apologists point to the generosity of the super-rich as evidence they're contributing as much to the nation's well-being as they did decades ago, when they paid a larger share of their earnings in taxes. Undoubtedly, super-rich family foundations, such as the Bill and Melinda Gates Foundation, have done much good. Super-rich philanthropic giving is on the rise. Here's another parallel with the Gilded Age of the late nineteenth century, when magnates like Andrew Carnegie and John D. Rockefeller established philanthropic institutions that survive today.

But a large portion of charitable deductions claimed by the wealthy go not to the poor. They go to culture palaces—operas, art museums, symphonies, and theaters—where the wealthy spend much of their leisure time, and to the universities they once attended and expect their children to attend (perhaps with the added inducement of knowing that these schools often practice affirmative action for "legacies"). I'm all in favor of supporting the arts and our universities, but let's face it: These aren't really charities, as most people understand the term. They're often investments in the lifestyles the wealthy already enjoy and want their children to have too. They're also investments in prestige—especially if they result in the family name being engraved on the new wing of an art museum or symphony hall.

It's their business how they donate their money, of course. But not entirely. In 2012, the U.S. Treasury would receive about $50 billion less than if the tax code didn't allow for charitable deductions. (Not incidentally, this is about the same

"CHARITABLE GIVING"

ediface complex

amount the government would spend in 2012 on Temporary Assistance for Needy Families, which is what remains of
welfare.) As with all tax deductions, this gap has to be filled
by other tax revenues or by spending cuts, or it just adds
to the deficit. I see why a contribution to, say, the Salvation
Army should be eligible for a charitable deduction. But why,
exactly, should a contribution to the Guggenheim Museum
or to Harvard University? A while ago, New York's Lincoln
Center had a gala supported by the charitable contributions
of hedge fund industry leaders, some of whom take home $1
billion a year. I may be missing something, but this doesn't
strike me as charity, either. Poor New Yorkers rarely attend
concerts at Lincoln Center. It turns out that only an estimated 10 percent of all charitable deductions are specifically
directed at the poor or organizations expressly dedicated
to helping the poor. In other words, the great switch of the
super-rich isn't into charity. It is, as I said, from supporting government through taxes to supporting government
through lending. As it turns out, that's not nearly enough
support.

THE DECLINE OF THE PUBLIC GOOD

A society is embodied most visibly in public institutions—
public schools, public libraries, public transportation, public
hospitals, public parks, public museums, public recreation,
public universities, and so on. But much of what's called
"public" today is increasingly private. Tolls are rising on
public highways and public bridges, as are tuitions at so-
called public universities and admission fees at public parks
and public museums. Much of the rest of what's considered

"public" has become so shoddy that those who can afford to do so find private alternatives.

As public schools deteriorate, the upper middle class and the wealthy send their kids to private ones. As public playgrounds and pools decay, the better-off buy memberships in private tennis and swimming clubs. As public hospitals decline, those who can afford it pay premium rates for private care. Gated communities and office parks now come with their own manicured lawns and walkways, security guards, and backup power systems.

Why the decline of public institutions? The financial squeeze on government at all levels since 2008 explains only part of it. The real story began thirty years ago. When almost all the gains from growth started going to the top, the better-off began shifting to private institutions. They simultaneously started to withdraw political support for public ones, using their political clout to reduce their tax payments. This created a vicious cycle of diminishing public revenues and deteriorating quality, spurring more flight from public institutions.

The great expansion of public institutions in America began in the early years of the twentieth century, when progressive reformers championed the idea that we all benefit from public goods. Excellent schools, roads, parks, playgrounds, and transit systems were meant to knit the new industrial society together, create better citizens, and generate widespread prosperity. Education, for example, was less a personal investment than a public good, improving the entire community and ultimately the nation. This logic was expanded upon in subsequent decades—through the Great Depression, World War II, and the Cold War. The "greatest generation" was bound together by mutual needs and

common threats. It invested in strong public institutions as bulwarks against, in turn, mass poverty, fascism, and communism.

Yet increasingly over the past three decades, "we're all in it together" has been replaced by "you're on your own." Global capital has outsourced American jobs abroad. As I've noted, the very rich have taken home almost unprecedented portions of total earnings while paying lower and lower tax rates. A new wave of immigrants has hit our shores, only to be condemned by demagogues who forget we are mostly a nation of immigrants. Not even Democrats any longer use the phrase "the public good." Public goods are now, at best, "public investments." Public institutions have morphed into "public-private partnerships," or, for Republicans, "vouchers."

In his standard stump speech the presidential candidate Mitt Romney charged that President Obama and the Democrats created an "entitlement society," and Romney called for an "opportunity" society. But he never explained how ordinary Americans would be able to take advantage of opportunities without good public schools, affordable higher education, good roads, and adequate health care.

Romney's so-called entitlements were mostly a mirage anyway. Medicare is the only entitlement growing faster than the gross domestic product (GDP), but that's because the cost of health care is growing faster than the economy. Social Security hasn't contributed to the budget deficit; it's had surpluses for years. Other safety nets are in tatters. Unemployment insurance reaches just 40 percent of the jobless these days. The only reason food stamps and other benefits for the poor spiked after 2008 is that more Americans fell into poverty after getting clobbered by the Great Recession that hit in that year.

Outside of defense, domestic discretionary spending is down sharply as a percentage of the economy. This spending is "discretionary" in that Congress decides how much to fund such programs in annual appropriations bills. So as the budget is squeezed, these programs are the first to be whittled back. Yet they include the most important things we do as a nation to invest in the future productivity of all our people. With declining state and local spending, total public spending on education, infrastructure, and basic research has dropped from 12 percent of GDP in the 1970s to less than 3 percent in 2011.

Most federal programs to help children and lower-income families are in this vulnerable category as well. Yet more than one in three young families with children (headed by someone thirty or under) were living in poverty in 2010, according to an analysis of census data by Northeastern University's Center for Labor Market Studies. That's the highest percentage on record. In 2011, according to the Agriculture Department, nearly one in four young children (23.6 percent) lived in a family that had difficulty affording sufficient food at some point during the year. An analysis of federal data by *The New York Times* showed the number of children receiving subsidized lunches rose to twenty-one million in 2011, up from eighteen million in 2006–2007. Nearly a dozen states experienced increases of 25 percent or more—signaling a surge in child poverty. Under federal rules, children from families with incomes up to 130 percent of the poverty line, $29,055 for a family of four, are eligible.

America is still in the gravitational pull of the worst economy since the Great Depression—with lower-income families and kids bearing the worst of it—and yet the nation is cutting programs Americans desperately need to get through it. Local family services are being terminated. Tens of thousands of social workers have been laid off. Cities and counties are reducing or eliminating their contributions to Head Start, which provides early childhood education to the children of low-income parents. It gets worse. The automatic budget trigger of January 2013 to cut the federal budget takes an even bigger whack at domestic discretionary spending. States no longer receive federal stimulus money—money that was used to fill gaps in state budgets over the last two years. The result is a downward cascade of budget cuts—from the federal government to state governments and then to local governments—that are hurting most Americans, but kids and lower-income families in particular.

In March 2012, Republicans in the House of Representatives approved a budget that would cut $3.3 trillion from low-income programs over the subsequent decade, according to the nonpartisan Center on Budget and Policy Priorities. The biggest cuts would be in Medicaid, providing health care for the nation's poor—forcing states to drop coverage for an estimated fourteen million to twenty-eight million low-income people. The Republican budget would also reduce food stamps for poor families by 17 percent ($133.5 billion) over the decade, leading to a significant increase in hunger—particularly among children. It would also reduce housing assistance, job training, and Pell grants for college tuition. In all, 62 percent of the budget cuts would come from low-income programs. Yet at the same time, the Republican budget would provide a substantial tax cut to the rich—who are already taking home an almost unprecedented share of the nation's total income.

Mitt Romney, the Republican presidential candidate, said he was "very supportive" of the plan. "It's a bold and exciting effort, an excellent piece of work, very much needed. . . . It's very consistent with what I put out earlier." Indeed. When the Center on Budget and Policy Priorities analyzed Romney's plan, it found that it would throw ten million low-income people off the benefits rolls for food stamps or cut benefits by thousands of dollars a year, or both. "These cuts would primarily affect very low-income families with children, seniors and people with disabilities," the center concluded. At the same time, Romney's tax plan would boost the incomes of America's wealthiest citizens. He would permanently extend George W. Bush's tax cuts, reduce corporate income tax rates, and eliminate the estate tax. These tax reductions would increase the incomes of people earning more than $1 million a year by an average of $295,874 annually, according to the nonpartisan Tax Policy Center.

By reducing government revenues, Romney's tax cuts would squeeze programs for the poor even further. Extending the Bush tax cuts would add $1.2 trillion to the nation's budget deficit in just two years. Oh, did I say that Romney and other Republicans also want to repeal President Obama's health-care law, thereby leaving fifty million Americans without health insurance?

Meanwhile, the nation has been cutting school budgets to shreds, even though the size of America's school-age population keeps growing. By 2015, an additional two million kids are expected to show up in our schools. Yet in 2012, twenty-three states reduced education spending, on top of cuts in 2011 and 2010. Education is one of the biggest expenses in state budgets. But states can't run deficits—almost every state constitution forbids it—and tax revenues during the prolonged downturn have not kept up. Nor has the federal government come to the aid of the states.

Arizona eliminated preschool for more than four thousand children and cut funding for books, computers, and other classroom supplies. California reduced kindergarten through twelfth grade aid to local school districts by billions of dollars and is cutting a variety of programs, including adult literacy instruction and help for high-needs students. Colorado and Georgia reduced public school spending nearly 5 percent from 2010; Illinois and Massachusetts, by 3 percent. Virginia's $700 million in cuts included funding for class-size reduction in kindergarten through third grade. The state of Washington suspended a program to reduce class size. Pennsylvania squeezed local budgets: Philadelphia laid off fourteen hundred teachers and staff; Carlisle used sheep to trim its playing fields.

Local communities can't make up the difference. As

housing values declined, revenues from local property taxes plummeted. This has meant even less money for schools and local family services. So thirty or more children are squeezed into ever more crowded classrooms with reduced school hours and shorter school weeks. Prekindergarten programs are being cut. Schools have even started to charge families for textbooks and extracurricular activities.

Meanwhile, at least forty-three states have cut funding for public colleges and universities and have increased tuitions and fees. As a result, many qualified young people are not able to attend. For example, the University of California, where I teach, has increased tuition by 32 percent and reduced freshman enrollment by twenty-three hundred students; the California State University system cut enrollment by forty thousand students. The Arizona' Board of Regents has approved in-state undergraduate tuition (tuition paid by students who are residents of the state) increases of between 9 and 20 percent as well as fee increases at the state's three public universities. Florida's public universities raised tuition 32 percent. New York's state university system increased resident undergraduate tuition by 14 percent. Texas cut funding for higher education by 5 percent, or $73 million. Washington reduced state funding for the University of Washington by 26 percent.

Because of these state cuts and tuition hikes, families and young people are absorbing more of the cost of higher education. The total amount of outstanding student debt is staggering, reaching over $1 trillion in 2012. That was more than the total of outstanding credit-card debt. Almost a third of students graduating from college are burdened with these debts, averaging $25,000 each. Punitive laws enforce repayment, and it is almost impossible to shed student loans in bankruptcy. There is no statute of limitations for non-repayment. Why have we allowed this to happen? Our young people—their capacities to think, understand, investigate, and innovate—are America's future. In the name of fiscal prudence we're endangering that future.

In a 2011 survey of thirty-four advanced nations by the Organization for Economic Cooperation and Development, our kids came in twenty-fifth in math, seventeenth in science, and fourteenth in reading. The average fifteen-year-old American student can't answer as many test questions correctly as the average fifteen-year-old student in Shanghai. America's biggest corporations don't seem to care about the deterioration of American education, because they're getting the talent they need all over the world. Many of them now have research and development operations in Europe and China, for example. America's wealthy and upper-middle-class families don't seem particularly worried, either. They have enough money to send their kids to good private schools and to pay high tuitions at private universities. But the rest of the nation is imperiled.

I'm not one of those who believes the only way to fix what's wrong with American education is to throw more money at it. We also need to make improvements in how we educate students. Judging teacher performance has to be squarely on the table, and teachers should be paid according to how well their students learn. We should experiment with vouchers whose worth is inversely related to family income. Universities have to tame their budgets for student amenities that have nothing to do with education. But nor can we educate our nation on the cheap. Considering the increases in our population of young people and their educational needs in the new global economy, more resources are surely necessary.

President Obama called this a "Sputnik moment," referring to the wake-up call to America by the Soviet's successful launch in the 1950s that resulted in the National Defense Education Act, training a whole generation of math and science teachers. Sadly, we're heading in the opposite direction. The budget agreement of 2012 invites even more federal budget cuts in public education. Pell grants that allow young people from poor families to attend college are already squeezed.

No wonder so many Americans feel that no matter how hard they or their children try, they can no longer get ahead. The game seems rigged because, increasingly, it is. We're losing public goods available to all, supported by taxes. In their place are private goods available mainly to the very rich. At the same time, the rich are paying less to support the public good. And more and more government expenditures are finding their way into bailouts, subsidies, and government contracts going to favored industries and their shareholders and executives.

There is something dreadfully wrong with this picture.

The Broken Basic Bargain

As I write this, jobs are starting to return, and America appears to be emerging from the deepest economic downturn we've experienced since the Great Depression. But the pay of most Americans is not returning—and that is the longer-term and more disturbing story. For most of the last century, the basic bargain at the heart of the American economy was that employers paid their workers enough to buy what American employers were selling. That basic bargain created a virtuous cycle of higher living standards, more jobs, and better wages. But for the last thirty years that basic bargain has been coming apart.

HENRY FORD

1863–
1947

In 1914, Henry Ford announced he was paying workers on his Model T assembly line $5 a day—three times what the typical factory employee earned at the time. *The Wall Street Journal* termed his action "an economic crime," but Ford knew it was a cunning business move. The higher wage turned Ford's autoworkers into customers who could afford to buy Model Ts. In two years Ford's profits more than doubled.

That was then. Now Ford Motor Company is paying its new hires about half what it paid its new employees a decade ago. Ford's newest workers earn about $14 an hour, in contrast to the $25 an hour earned by new Ford workers in 2002 (adjusted for inflation). Ford also gives today's new recruits a maximum of four weeks of paid time off a year; Ford workers used to get five weeks. And instead of receiving a guaranteed $3,000-a-month pension when they retire at age sixty, new hires must build their own "personal retirement plans," to which Ford contributes less than $2,000 a year.

It's the same story across America. At GE, new hires earn $12 to $19 an hour, versus $21 to $32 an hour earned by workers who started at GE a decade or more ago. According to the Commerce Department, employee pay is down to the smallest share of the economy since the government began collecting wage and salary figures data in 1929. Meanwhile, corporate profits now constitute the largest share of the economy since 1929.

In case you forgot, 1929 was the year of the crash that ushered in the Great Depression. In the years leading up to that crash, most employers forgot Henry Ford's example. The wages of most American workers remained stagnant. The gains of economic growth went mainly into corporate profits and into the pockets of the very rich. American families maintained their standard of living by going deeper into debt. In 1929 the debt bubble popped.

Sound familiar? It should. The same thing happened in the years leading up to the crash of 2008. And more recent data show the trends continuing. In other words, we still haven't learned the essential lesson of the two big economic crashes of the last seventy-five years: when the economy becomes too lopsided—disproportionately benefiting corporate owners and top executives vis-à-vis average workers—it tips over.

The real reason the American economy tanked in 2008, and why we're still struggling to recover, is that the basic bargain has been broken. The big economic news isn't the slow return of jobs. It's the continuing drop in pay. Most of the jobs we've gained since the Great Recession pay less than the jobs lost during it. An analysis from the National Employment Law Project shows that the biggest losses were in jobs paying between $19.05 and $31.40 an hour; the biggest increases have been in jobs paying an average of $9.03 to $12.91 an hour.

For several years now, conservative economists have blamed high unemployment on the purported fact that many Americans have priced themselves out of the global/high-tech jobs market. So if we want more jobs, they say, we'll need to accept lower wages and benefits. That's exactly what Americans have been doing. More and more Americans are retaining their jobs by settling for lower pay or going without cost-of-living increases. Or they've lost a higher-paying job and have taken one that pays less. Or they've joined the great army of contingent workers, self-employed "consultants," temps, and contract workers—without health-care benefits, pensions, job security, or decent wages.

All told, the decade starting in 2001 was the worst decade for American workers in a century. According to Commerce Department data, private sector wage gains even lagged behind wage gains during the decade of the Great Depression (4 percent between 2001 and 2011, adjusted for inflation, versus 5 percent from 1929 to 1939). Conservatives say that's still not enough, which is why unions have to be busted—and why Republican governors and legislators are trying to pass so-called right-to-work laws banning employment contracts requiring employees to join a union and pay union dues. Without such a requirement there's no reason for any particular worker to join a union, because he can get the bargaining advantages of unionization without paying for them—which in turn destroys unions, exactly the point. In 2012, Indiana enacted the nation's first right-to-work law in more than a decade and the first ever in the heavily unionized upper Midwest.

The current attack on public sector workers logically follows. As the pay and benefits of workers in the private sector continue to drop, Republicans claim public sector workers now take home more generous pay and benefits packages than private sector workers. It's not true on the wage side if you control for level of education, but it wasn't even true on the benefits side until private sector benefits fell off a cliff. Meanwhile, all across America, public sector workers are being "furloughed," which is a nice word for not collecting any pay for weeks at a time.

It's no great feat to create lots of lousy jobs. A few years ago the Republican congresswoman Michele Bachmann remarked that if the minimum wage were repealed, "we could potentially virtually wipe out unemployment completely because we would be able to offer jobs at whatever level." If you accept her logic, why stop there? After all, slavery was a full-employment system.

Conservative economists have it wrong. The underlying problem isn't that most Americans have priced themselves out of the global/high-tech labor market. It's that most Americans are receiving a smaller share of the American pie. This not only is bad for the majority but also hobbles the economy. Lower incomes mean less overall demand for goods and services, which translates into lower wages in the future. The basic bargain once recognized that average workers are also consumers and that their paychecks keep the economy going. We can't have a full-fledged recovery and we can't sustain a healthy economy until that bargain is restored.

What happened to America? Why and how did we come apart?

What Went Wrong

It's estimated the economy would grow by 2 percent in 2012, which is peanuts. The deeper the economic hole we've been in, the faster we need to grow in order to get back on track. Given the depth of the hole we fell into in 2008, we would need the economy to be growing by 4–6 percent in 2012 and at least that fast in 2013. Consider that in 1934, when the economy began emerging from the bottom of the Great Depression, it grew 7.7 percent. The next year it grew more than 8 percent. In 1936 it grew a whopping 14.1 percent.

The U.S. economy won't really bounce back until America's surge toward inequality is reversed. When so much income goes to the top, the middle class doesn't have enough purchasing power to keep the economy going without sinking ever more deeply into debt—which, as we've seen, ends badly. No economy can run mainly on the spending of the very wealthy. The richest 5 percent of Americans spend only about half of what they earn, which isn't surprising. Being rich means you've got just about everything you want and need. The 5 percent of Americans with the highest incomes accounted for 37 percent of all consumer purchases in 2012, according to Moody's Analytics. Yet the spending of the richest 5 percent alone will not lead to that virtuous cycle of more jobs and higher living standards. Nor can we rely on exports to fill the gap. It is impossible for every large economy, including that of the United States, to become a net exporter. An economy so dependent on the spending of a few is also prone to great booms and busts. The rich splurge and speculate when their savings are doing well, but they pull back when the values of their assets tumble. Sound familiar?

Even if by some chance Washington enacts another big stimulus while the Federal Reserve keeps interest rates near zero, these policies can't work without a middle class capable of spending. Pump priming helps only when a well contains enough water.

Look back over the last hundred years and you'll see the

pattern. During periods when the very rich took home a much smaller proportion of total income—as in the Great Prosperity between 1947 and 1977—the nation as a whole grew faster, and median wages surged. The basic bargain ensured that the pay of American workers coincided with their output. In effect, the vast middle class received an increasing share of the benefits of economic growth. America created that virtuous cycle in which an ever-growing middle class had the ability to consume more goods and services, which created more and better jobs, thereby stoking demand. The rising tide did in fact lift all boats. On the other hand, during periods when the very rich took home a larger proportion—as between 1918 and 1933, and in the Great Regression from 1981 to the present day—growth slowed, median wages stagnated, and the nation suffered giant downturns.

It's no mere coincidence that over the last century the top earners' share of the nation's total income peaked twice, in 1928 and 2007—the two years just preceding the biggest downturns.

In the late 1970s, the middle class began to weaken. The two lines began to diverge: Output per hour—a measure of productivity—continued to rise. But real hourly compensation was left in the dust. This was mainly because new technologies—container ships, satellite communications, eventually computers and the Internet—started to undermine any American job that could be automated or done more cheaply abroad. Factories remaining in the United States have shed workers as they automated. So has the service sector. But contrary to popular mythology, trade and technology have not reduced the overall number of American jobs; their more profound effect has been on pay. As I noted, jobs slowly returned from the depths of the Great Recession, but

The **GREAT**
↑ **PROSPERITY**
1947-1977

Top 1% gets declining
share of total
income +
wealth

WAGES UP
Productivity UP
employment UP
middle class gets
increasing share

Compare

The **GREAT**
↓ **REGRESSION**
1981 - 2007
and beyond?

Top 1% gets growing
share of total income
+ wealth

WAGES
Productivity
employment
middle-class
share

ALL DOWN

in order to get them, many workers had to accept lower pay than before.

Over the last three and a half decades, middle-class families continued to spend, the breakdown of the basic bargain notwithstanding. Their spending was at first enabled by the flow of women into the workforce. In the 1960s, only 12 percent of married women with children under the age of six were working for pay; by the late 1990s, 55 percent were in the paid workforce. When that way of life stopped generating enough income, Americans went deeper into debt. From the late 1990s to 2007, the typical household debt grew by a third. As long as housing values continued to rise, it seemed a painless way to get additional money. Eventually, of course, the bubble burst. That ended the middle class's remarkable ability to keep spending in the face of near-stagnant wages.

The puzzle is why so little was done during those years to help deal with the subversion of the economic power of the middle class. With the continued gains from economic growth, the nation could have enabled more people to become the kinds of problem solvers and innovators that could summon higher pay—starting with early childhood education, better public schools, expanded access to higher education, and more efficient public transportation. The nation might also have enlarged safety nets—by having unemployment insurance cover part-time work, by giving transition assistance to those moving to new jobs in new locations, by creating insurance for communities that lost a major employer. And we could have ensured that our workforce and their families were healthy by making Medicare available to anyone. Big companies could have been required to pay severance to American workers they let go, and train them for new jobs. The minimum wage could have been pegged at

half the median wage, and we could have insisted that the
foreign nations we trade with do the same so that all citizens
could share in gains from trade. We could have raised taxes
on the rich and cut them for poorer Americans.

But starting in the late 1970s, and with increasing fer-
vor over the next three decades, government did just the
opposite. It deregulated and privatized. It cut spending on
infrastructure as a percentage of the national economy and
shifted more of the costs of public higher education to families. It shredded safety nets. And it allowed companies to bust
unions and threaten employees who tried to organize. Fewer
than 7 percent of private sector workers are now unionized.
Meanwhile, as I've noted, the top income tax rate was halved
to 35 percent, and many of the nation's richest were allowed
to treat their income as capital gains subject to no more than
15 percent tax. Inheritance taxes that affected only the topmost 1.5 percent of earners were sliced. Yet at the same time
sales and payroll taxes—which are more painful to those with
modest paychecks—were increased.

Most telling of all, Washington deregulated Wall Street
while insuring it against major losses. In so doing, it allowed
finance, which until then had been the servant of American industry, to become its master, demanding short-term
profits over long-term growth and raking in an ever-larger
portion of the nation's profits. By 2007, financial companies
accounted for more than 40 percent of American corporate
profits and almost as great a percentage of pay, up from 10
percent during the Great Prosperity, the three decades after
World War II when the middle class expanded and prosperity was widely shared.

Some say the regressive lurch occurred because Americans
lost confidence in government. But this argument has cause

and effect backward. The tax revolts that thundered across America starting in the late 1970s were not so much ideological revolts against government—Americans still wanted all the government services they had before, and then some—as revolts against paying more taxes on incomes that had stagnated. Inevitably, government services deteriorated and government deficits exploded, confirming the public's growing cynicism about government's doing anything right.

Others say we couldn't have reversed the consequences of globalization and technological change. Yet the experiences of other nations, like Germany, suggest otherwise. Since the mid-1990s, Germany has grown faster than the United States, and the gains from that growth have been more widely spread. While Americans' average hourly pay has risen only 6 percent since 1985, adjusted for inflation, German workers' pay has risen almost 30 percent. At the same time, the top 1 percent of German households takes home only about 11 percent of all income—the same as in 1970. And although in 2012 Germany was hit by the debt crisis of its neighbors, its unemployment was still below where it was when the financial crisis started in 2007. Germany has done it mainly by focusing like a laser on education (with regard to math scores, German students continue to extend their lead over American students) and by maintaining strong labor unions.

The real reason for America's Great Regression starting in 1981 has been political, not economic. As income and wealth became more concentrated in fewer hands, American politics reverted to what Marriner S. Eccles, a former chairman of the Federal Reserve, described in the 1920s, when people "with great economic power had an undue influence in making the rules of the economic game." With hefty cam-

paign contributions and platoons of lobbyists and public relations spinners, America's executive class has secured lower
tax rates while resisting reforms that would spread the gains
from growth to more Americans.

But it's unlikely that the plutocrats can retain their political clout forever. So many people have been hit by job losses,
sagging incomes, and declining home values that Americans will eventually become mobilized. The question is not
whether but when. Perhaps the Occupier movement marks
the beginning. Americans have summoned the political will
to take back our economy before, in even bleaker times. As
the historian James Truslow Adams defined the American
dream when he coined the term at the depths of the Great
Depression, what we seek is "a land in which life should be
better and richer and fuller for every man."

Why Big Corporations Won't Lead the Way

Republicans want to rely on big American corporations to
solve our economic problems and to reduce the size and
scope of government. But the prosperity of America's big
businesses has become disconnected from the prosperity
of most Americans. Without a government that's focused
on more and better jobs, we're left with global corporations
that don't give a damn. And American corporations are increasingly global, with less and less stake in America.

According to the Commerce Department, American-
based global corporations added 2.4 million workers abroad
in the first decade of this century while cutting their American workforce by 2.9 million. Between 2009 and 2011, the
thirty-five biggest U.S. companies added 113,000 Ameri-

can jobs but almost three times that many jobs (333,000) abroad, according to a survey by *The Wall Street Journal*. Nearly 60 percent of their revenue growth came from outside the United States. Apple employs 43,000 people in the United States but contracts with over 700,000 workers abroad. It makes iPhones in China both because wages are low there and because Apple's Chinese contractor can quickly mobilize workers from company dormitories at almost any hour of the day or night.

American companies aren't creating just routine jobs overseas. They're also creating good high-tech jobs there and doing more of their research and development abroad. The share of research and development spending going to their foreign subsidiaries rose from 9 percent in 1989 to almost 16 percent in 2009. The National Science Foundation (NSF) warns that the United States is quickly losing ground in research. China's share of global research and development now tops ours. One big reason, according to the NSF, is that American firms nearly doubled their research and development investments in Asia over the last decade.

That's because China has a national economic strategy designed to make it the economic powerhouse of the future. China wants to create the technologies and the jobs of the future, and it has been pouring money into world-class research centers designed to lure American corporations along with their engineers and scientists. The Chinese are intent on learning as much as they can from American corporations and then going beyond them—as they already have in solar and electric-battery technologies. They're also pouring money into education at all levels. In the last dozen years they've built twenty universities, each intended to become the equivalent of MIT. American corporations are happy to play along because China has the biggest consumer market in the world, to which every American company wants access.

At the 2011 summit between the Chinese president, Hu Jintao, and President Obama, China agreed to buy $45 billion of American exports. President Obama said the agreement would create more American jobs, but in fact it would create more profits for American companies and relatively few new jobs for Americans. Nearly half of the deal was for two hundred Boeing aircraft whose parts would be manufactured all over the world. The rest involved agricultural commodities that don't require much U.S. labor (because American agribusiness is highly automated) and chemical and high-tech goods that are even less labor-intensive. American corporations signed up for deals with China involving energy and aviation manufacturing, but much of the work would be done in China.

American companies don't care, as long as the deals help their bottom lines. An Apple executive told *The New York Times,* "We don't have an obligation to solve America's problems. Our only obligation is making the best product possible." He might have added, *and showing profits big enough to continually increase our share price.* If Apple or any other big American company can make a product best and cheapest in China or anywhere else, then that's where it'll do it. I don't blame the companies. American corporations are in business to make profits and boost their share value, not to create good American jobs. That's the form of capitalism we practice, in contrast with China's "state-run" capitalism.

The real problem is that American firms also have huge clout in Washington. They maintain legions of lobbyists and are pouring boatloads of money into political campaigns.

After the Supreme Court's decision in *Citizens United v. Federal Election Commission,* there's no limit. (That ruling allows corporations to give unlimited amounts of money to candidates.) Their clout would extend into the Obama White House. The president's own Council on Jobs and Competitiveness would be chaired by Jeffrey Immelt, CEO of GE, and comprise CEOs of other big American corporations.

But the indifference if not outright opposition of big American corporations to higher wages and better jobs in America hobbles the development of a national economic strategy to generate both. GE, for example, has been creating more jobs outside the United States than in it. A decade ago, most of GE's employees were American; today, the majority are non-American. Fifty-three percent of GE's $150.2 billion in revenue in 2011, from all sources, came from abroad (up from 35 percent only a decade before). And like other major corporations, GE has been shifting more of its research to China. In 2011 it announced a $500 million expansion of its research and development facilities there on top of a $2 billion initial investment. GE's joint venture with Aviation Industry Corporation of China, to develop new integrated avionics systems (which presumably will find their way into Boeing planes), will be based in Shanghai.

It should come as no surprise that the President's Council on Jobs and Competitiveness called for lower corporate taxes and fewer regulations. It also called for repeal of the anti-corporate-looting provisions enacted by Congress in 2002 in response to the Enron fiasco, arguing that they impede growth and hiring. But lower corporate taxes and fewer regulations won't bring good jobs to America. They might lower the costs of production here, but global companies can always find even lower costs somewhere else around the world. America's corporate elite also wants China to raise the value of its currency so that everything it buys from us is cheaper and everything we buy from it is more expensive. But even if our currencies were better balanced, China would still come out ahead. We'd have more jobs because our exports would be more attractive in world markets, but those jobs would summon fewer goods from around the world. A lower-valued dollar makes everything else we buy from the rest of the world more expensive, so we in effect become poorer.

Global corporations will create jobs wherever around the world they can get the best return—either where wages are lowest or where productivity is highest or both. America can't and shouldn't try to compete on the basis of low wages; that's a recipe for a continuously declining standard of living. Global companies will create good, high-wage jobs in the United States only if Americans are productive enough and clever enough to summon them. Yet the sad truth is that a large and growing portion of our workforce is handicapped by deteriorating schools, unaffordable college tuitions, decaying infrastructure, worsening health and rising health-care costs, and diminishing basic research. All of this is putting us on a glide path toward even lousier jobs and lower wages. And we have no national plan to reverse any of this.

Instead of a national economic strategy to make these investments in our people, we have a hodgepodge of tax breaks and corporate welfare crafted by American-based global corporations to maximize their profits. They'll do and make things in China and give the Chinese their know-how when that's the best way to boost the corporations' bottom lines, and they'll utilize research and development wherever around the world it will deliver the biggest bang for the dollar. Meanwhile, deficit hawks in Congress are cutting pub-licly supported research and development. And cash-starved states are cutting K–12 education and slashing the budgets of their great public research universities.

China has a national economic strategy designed to create more and better jobs. We have global corporations designed to make money for their shareholders. No contest.

THE CONTINUING CLOUT OF THE STREET

Wall Street, meanwhile, has been using its lobbying power to water down regulations emerging from the Dodd-Frank financial reform law of 2010. The Street says Dodd-Frank is overkill. The reality is just the opposite: Dodd-Frank is too weak.

The European debt crisis, for example, isn't a problem for America's real economy. Whatever happens to Greece or other deeply indebted European governments, America's exports to Europe will not dry up. In any event, those ex-ports are small relative to the size of the U.S. economy. If you want to find the real reason for concern in the United States about what's happening in Europe, follow the money. If Greece defaults on its debts, Italy and Spain—the next weakest borrowers—will have to pay higher interest rates on their own debts, pushing one or both of them to the brink. A default by either Italy or Spain would have roughly the same effect on our financial system as the implosion of Lehman Brothers in 2008—that is, financial chaos. It could eas-ily pummel German and French banks, to which big Wall Street banks have lent a bundle. The Street has also bet on or insured all sorts of derivatives—in effect, bets placed on the outcomes of other trades—emanating from Europe, on energy, currency, interest rates, and foreign exchange swaps. If a German or French bank goes down, the ripple effects are incalculable.

The oracles of Wall Street said they weren't worried, because most of the Street's exposure to European banks was insured through "credit-default swaps" that would offset any losses. Wall Street's amnesia was breathtaking. Just four years before, AIG nearly collapsed because it couldn't make payments on its swap contracts that were supposed to insure big Wall Street banks against losses on their bets. American taxpayers had to bail out AIG as well as the big banks. One of the many ironies surrounding Wall Street's equanimity in the face of the European debt crisis was that some badly indebted European nations (Ireland is the best example) went deeply into debt in the first place by bailing out their banks from the crisis that began on Wall Street. Full circle.

You don't have to be an Occupier to conclude the Street is still out of control, rigged to benefit the biggest players (including the Street's biggest banks) at the expense of everyone else. In the summer of 2011, after Groupon selected Goldman Sachs, Morgan Stanley, and Credit Suisse to underwrite its initial public offering, the trio valued Groupon at a generous $30 billion. Subsequent accounting and disclosure problems showed this estimate to be absurdly high. But the banks didn't care a whit. The higher the valuation, the fatter their fees. When Facebook was about to go public in the spring of 2012, the big banks thought the initial price was too high, given what they thought the company would be earning in the future, and they shared their assessment with their major customers. But small investors didn't get the word, and as Facebook's shares tumbled, they lost money.

Or consider the collapse of MF Global, a Wall Street firm that gambled in financial futures, bet wrong on sovereign debt, and lost between $1.2 billion and $1.6 billion of its customers' money. Those funds were supposed to have been held separately, but MF Global and other firms trading futures contracts have few safeguards to protect customer money and don't even have to inform customers about where their money is.

The near meltdown of the Street in 2008 seems to have had no effect on the Street's subsequent behavior. Look at the fancy footwork by Bank of America (BofA) when hit by a credit downgrade in the fall of 2011. BofA avoided higher charges by simply moving the risky derivatives that had triggered the downgrade from its Merrill Lynch unit to a retail subsidiary flush with insured deposits. The subsidiary has a higher credit rating because those deposits are insured by the Federal Deposit Insurance Corporation (that is, you and me and our fellow citizens). Result: BofA improved its bottom line, at the expense of American taxpayers.

Wasn't this supposed to be illegal? Didn't we learn a thing from the debacle of 2008? Apparently not. In May 2012, Jamie Dimon, chairman and CEO of JPMorgan Chase, the nation's largest bank by assets, announced the bank had lost $2 billion to $3 billion in trades because of excessively risky bets that were "poorly executed" and "poorly monitored," the result of "many errors," "sloppiness," and "bad judgment." But not to worry, said Dimon. "We will admit it, we will fix it and move on."

Ever since the start of the banking crisis in 2008, Dimon had been arguing that more government regulation of Wall Street was unnecessary. In 2011 he vehemently and loudly opposed the so-called Volcker Rule, itself a watered-down version of the old Glass-Steagall Act—the Depression-era law that had separated investment banking (betting in the financial casino) from commercial banking (taking in deposits and lending them out). Glass-Steagall's repeal in 1999 had allowed bankers to place large bets with other people's money—and make huge windfalls for themselves. It also led to the near meltdown of the Street in 2008. Even then the Street fought against resurrecting Glass-Steagall, accepting the Volcker Rule as a compromise. But Dimon had insisted even the Volcker Rule went too far. It would unnecessarily impinge on derivative trading (the lucrative practice of making bets on bets) and hedging (using some bets to offset the risks of other bets).

Dimon argued the financial system could be trusted, that the near meltdown of 2008 was a perfect storm that would never happen again. "Most of the bad actors are gone," he said. "Off-balance-sheet businesses are virtually obliterated," "money market funds are far more transparent," and "most very exotic derivatives are gone." JPMorgan's lobbyists and lawyers then did everything in their power to eviscerate the Volcker Rule—creating exceptions, exemptions, and loopholes that effectively allow any big bank to go on doing most of the derivative trading it was doing before the near meltdown. By the time of Dimon's announcement of JPMorgan's trading losses, the rule had morphed into almost three hundred pages of regulatory mumbo jumbo and still hadn't been finalized.

In light of all this, Dimon's promise in May 2012, after revealing billions of dollars of losses from risky trades, that JPMorgan would "fix it and move on" was not reassuring.

Here we were—less than four years after a banking crisis had forced American taxpayers to bail out the Street, caused home values to plunge by more than 30 percent and pushed millions of homeowners underwater, threatened or diminished the savings of millions more, and sent the entire American economy hurtling into the worst downturn since the Great Depression—and JPMorgan recapitulated the whole debacle with the same kinds of errors, sloppiness, and bad judgment, and the same excessively risky, poorly executed, and poorly monitored trades, that had caused the crisis in the first place.

JPMorgan's losses had been mounting for at least six weeks, according to the bank. Where was the new transparency that was supposed to allow regulators to catch these things before they got out of hand? Where were the regulators who were supposed to be "embedded" in the big banks in order to stop such excessively risky trades from occurring? Several weeks before Dimon's announcement, there had been rumors about a London-based JPMorgan trader making huge high-stakes bets, causing excessive volatility in derivatives markets. When asked about it at the time, Dimon called it "a complete tempest in a teapot." Using the same argument he had used to fend off regulation of derivatives, he told investors that "every bank has a major portfolio" and "in those portfolios you make investments that you think are wise to offset your exposures."

Meanwhile, even the portion of the Dodd-Frank law that was supposed to be in effect was barely being enforced. That's because the agencies charged with enforcing it, including the Securities and Exchange Commission, didn't have enough money or staff to do the job. The Street's Washington lobbyists had made sure Congress didn't appropriate even these bare necessities. By late 2012 several of these agencies still lacked directors or commissioners. Ironically, many of the business leaders who blamed the sluggish economy on "regulatory uncertainty" were the same ones who kept financial regulation in limbo. A senior vice president of the Chamber of Commerce told *The New York Times,* "Uncertainty among companies about the rules of the road is keeping a lot of capital on the sidelines." Yes, and the Chamber of Commerce was among the groups most responsible for maintaining uncertainty about Dodd-Frank's final regulations.

The problem isn't excessive greed. If you took the greed out of Wall Street, all you'd have left is pavement. The problem is the Street's excessive power. Wall Street is the richest and most powerful industry in America with the closest ties to the federal government, routinely supplying Treasury secretaries and economic advisers who share its worldview and its financial interests and routinely bankrolling congressional kingpins. How else can you explain why the Street was bailed out with no strings attached? Or why taxpayers didn't get equity in the banks we bailed out—as Warren Buffett got when he bailed out Goldman Sachs—so when the banks became profitable again, we didn't get any of the upside gains? Or why no criminal charges have been brought against any major Wall Street figure—despite the effluvium of frauds, deceptions, malfeasance, and nonfeasance in the years leading up to the crash and subsequent bailout? Or why Dodd-Frank is being eviscerated?

Since Dodd-Frank was enacted, Wall Street has spent as

much on lobbyists and what amount to political payoffs designed to stop the law's implementation as it did trying to
water down the law in the first place. The six largest banks
spent $29.4 million on lobbying in 2010, and even more
in 2011. According to the Center for Public Integrity, the
Street and other financial institutions hired roughly three
thousand lobbyists to fight Dodd-Frank—more than five
lobbyists for every member of Congress. They hired almost
the same number to delay, weaken, or otherwise prevent its
implementation.

As a presidential candidate, Mitt Romney, who promised to seek repeal of Dodd-Frank if elected, received more
money from securities, investment, banking, and other
bastions of finance than from any other industry. Barack
Obama, having pushed Dodd-Frank, received far less of
Wall Street beneficence in his bid for reelection. Nonetheless, big finance has remained the single largest source of
cash for the national Democratic Party's various campaign
committees, contributing even more than the traditionally
pro-Democratic entertainment industry.

Yet the largest part of the Street's political efforts are almost entirely hidden from view, occurring within regulatory
and legal processes that run beneath Washington like a giant
system of underground plumbing. In 2012 the Street's biggest lobbying groups filed a lawsuit against the Commodity
Futures Trading Commission seeking to overturn its new
rule limiting speculative trading in food, oil, and other com-
modities. Wall Street profits greatly from these bets, but
they raise consumer costs—another redistribution from the
middle class and the poor to the top. The Street argued the
commission's cost-benefit analysis wasn't adequate. It was

a clever ploy because there's no clear legal standard for an "adequate" weighing of costs and benefits of financial regulations since both are so difficult to measure. And putting the question into the laps of federal judges gave the Street a major tactical advantage because the Street has almost an infinite amount of money to hire so-called experts who will say benefits have been exaggerated and costs underestimated, while the commission's budget is limited.

The Street used the same ploy in 2011 after the Securities and Exchange Commission (SEC) tried to make it easier for shareholders to nominate company directors. Wall Street argued that the SEC's cost-benefit analysis was inadequate. In July 2011, a federal appeals court—inundated by Wall Street lawyers and hired-gun "experts"—agreed with the Street. So much for shareholder rights.

Obviously, government should weigh the costs against the benefits of anything it does. But when it comes to regulating Wall Street, one big cost doesn't make it into any individual weighing: the public's mounting distrust of our entire economic system, generated by the Street's repeated abuse of the public's trust. Wall Street's shenanigans have convinced a large portion of America that the economic game is rigged. Yet capitalism depends on trust. Without trust, people avoid even sensible economic risks. They also begin trading in gray markets and black markets. They think that if the big guys cheat in big ways, they may as well begin cheating in small ways. And when they think the game is rigged, they're easy prey for political demagogues with fast tongues and dumb ideas.

Wall Street has blanketed America in a miasma of cynicism, and much of it is directed against Wall Street. The

Street has only itself to blame. It should have welcomed new financial regulations as a means of restoring public trust. Instead, it's been busily shredding new regulations and making the public more distrustful than ever. The cost of such cynicism has leeched deep into America, finding expression in Tea Partiers and Occupiers and millions of others who think the Street has sold us out.

Whom Is the Economy For, Anyway?

All of this raises the basic question of whom the economy is for. Surely it's not just for a few Wall Street executives and traders or a handful of managers of hedge funds and private-equity funds, and not just for big corporations and their CEOs. The success of our economy cannot be measured by how fast the GDP grows or how high the Dow Jones Industrial Average rises, because in an economy like ours very few of the gains from growth or from a rising stock market are trickling down to most people.

The economy's success can't be measured by the unemployment rate, either. As I've emphasized, that rate doesn't take account of declining wages. Nor does it account for all the people who have become too discouraged to look for work because there are no jobs for them, and all those who are working part-time who want and need full-time jobs, or the growing ranks of contract workers, temporary workers, and others living from paycheck to paycheck with no job security at all.

Our economy's success can't even be measured by whether average incomes are turning upward. An average can disguise what's happening to the majority because averages are pulled up by the top, and when the top is exceptionally high, the average can be far better than what most people experience. Shaquille O'Neal and I have an average height of six feet.

Even if most Americans are able to buy more, our lives will not improve if our schools, parks, roads, air and water, and other public goods continue to deteriorate. We won't feel better off if our workplaces are unsafe, if we have no regular access to medical care, or if the cost of a major illness can wipe out our savings. And our lives will not be better if our democracy is dying, replaced by a system mostly responsive to big corporations and wealthy individuals.

An economy should exist for the people who inhabit it, not the other way around. The purpose of an economy is to provide everyone with opportunities to live full, happy, and productive lives. Yet when most people come to view the economic game as rigged, this most basic purpose cannot be achieved. It is impossible to live happily in a society that seems fundamentally unfair or to live well in a nation rife with anger and cynicism.

Part Two

The Rise of the Regressive Right

People who call themselves conservative Republicans offer one option for what to do about all this, but their option would make matters worse. Their goal is not to conserve the best of what we now have; it is to return America to a time long before we achieved it. In truth, their agenda is regressive rather than conservative. They believe in social Darwinism, and many will stop at nothing to get their way. Their strategy is to divide working Americans, to talk about private morality instead of public morality, and to convince Americans of the truth of a few very big lies.

The Rebirth of Social Darwinism

A fundamental war has been waged in this nation since its founding between progressive forces pushing us forward

and regressive forces pulling us backward. We are in that battle once again.

Progressives believe in openness, equal opportunity, and tolerance. Progressives assume we're all in it together: We all benefit from public investments in schools and health care and infrastructure. And we all do better with strong safety nets, reasonable constraints on Wall Street and big business, and a truly progressive tax system. Progressives worry when the rich and privileged become powerful enough to undermine democracy.

Regressives take the opposite positions. In 2012 their most prominent members were the House majority leader, Eric Cantor; the House budget chief, Paul Ryan; the former Speaker Newt Gingrich; the former senator Rick Santorum; the former majority leader Dick Armey; Governor Rick Perry of Texas; Representative Michele Bachmann of Minnesota; the former Alaska governor Sarah Palin; Representative Ron Paul of Texas; and the former Massachusetts governor and Republican presidential candidate Mitt Romney; along with the antigovernment guru Grover Norquist, several Fox News anchors, the Supreme Court justices Antonin Scalia and Clarence Thomas, and the Republican strategist Karl Rove. Behind them—funding their activities but carefully remaining out of the spotlight—are the media mogul Rupert Murdoch, the billionaires Charles and David Koch, and a coterie of other big-moneyed interests on and off Wall Street who view the regressive movement as their best means of maintaining their power and privilege and accumulating even more.

Many of these people would like to return America to the 1920s—before Social Security, unemployment insurance, labor laws, the minimum wage, Medicare and Medicaid, worker safety laws, the Environmental Protection Act, the Glass-Steagall Act, the Securities Exchange Act, and the Voting Rights Act. In the 1920s, Wall Street was unfettered, the rich grew far richer and everyone else went deep into debt, and the nation closed its doors to immigrants. These regressives also want to resurrect the classical economics of the 1920s—the view that economic downturns are best addressed by doing nothing until the "rot" is purged out of the system (as Andrew Mellon, Herbert Hoover's Treasury secretary, so decorously put it).

Many would even like to take the nation back to the late nineteenth century—before the federal income tax, antitrust laws, the Pure Food and Drug Act, and the Federal Reserve. It was a time when so-called robber barons—railroad, financial, and oil titans—ran the country; a time of wrenching squalor for the many and mind-numbing wealth for the few, when the federal government was small, the Fed and the Internal Revenue Service had yet to be invented, state laws

determined worker safety and hours, evolution was still considered contentious, immigrants were almost all European,
big corporations and robber barons ran the government, the
poor were desperate, and the rich lived like old-world aris-
tocrats. It was an era when the nation was mesmerized by
the doctrine of free enterprise but few Americans actually
enjoyed much freedom. The financier Jay Gould, the railroad
magnate Cornelius Vanderbilt, and the oil tycoon John D.
Rockefeller controlled much of American industry; the gap
between rich and poor had turned into a chasm; urban slums
festered; children worked long hours in factories; women
couldn't vote, and black Americans were subject to Jim
Crow; and the lackeys of the rich literally deposited sacks of
money on desks of pliant legislators.

Most tellingly, it was a time when the ideas of William
Graham Sumner, a professor of political and social science at Yale, dominated American social thought. Today's
Republican right deploys the same social Darwinism that
Sumner used more than a century ago to justify the brazen
inequality of the Gilded Age: survival of the fittest. Don't
help the poor or the unemployed or anyone who's fallen on
bad times, they say, because this only encourages laziness.
America will be strong only if we reward the rich and pun-
ish the needy. Sumner brought Charles Darwin's thinking

WILLIAM GRAHAM
SUMNER

1840-
1910

to America and twisted it into
a theory to fit the times. Few
Americans living today have
read any of Sumner's writings, but they had an electri-
fying effect on America during the last three decades of
the nineteenth century.

To Sumner and his followers, life was a competitive struggle in which only the fittest could and should survive, and through this struggle societies became stronger over time. A correlate of this principle was that government should do little or nothing to help those in need because that would interfere with natural selection.

Listen to today's Republicans and you hear a continuous regurgitation of Sumner. "Civilization has a simple choice," Sumner wrote in the 1880s. It's either "liberty, inequality, survival of the fittest" or "not-liberty, equality, survival of the unfittest. The former carries society forward and favors all its best members; the latter carries society downwards and favors all its worst members." Sound familiar?

Mitt Romney isn't as regressive as some, but like Herbert Hoover, he doesn't want the government to do much of anything about unemployment. As I said earlier, in the 2012 presidential campaign Romney accused President Obama of having created an "entitlement society" that has fostered a culture of dependence. Romney thinks government shouldn't try to help distressed homeowners but instead let the market "hit the bottom." And he is dead set against raising taxes on millionaires, relying on the standard Republican rationale that millionaires create jobs and that benefits trickle down.

Rick Santorum, another prominent Republican who was among the front-runners in the GOP 2012 presidential primary, accused the president of getting America hooked on "the narcotic of dependency" and alleged the reason we have high unemployment is that people are deliberately staying out of the workforce in order to get unemployment benefits. "When you have ninety-nine weeks of unemployment benefits and a variety of other social safety-net programs, people can make choices that they otherwise wouldn't make."

Newt Gingrich, another primary contender, not only echoes Sumner's thoughts but mimics his reputed arrogance. Gingrich says we must reward "entrepreneurs" (by which he means anyone who has made a pile of money) and warns us not to "coddle" people in need. In the GOP primary he called laws against child labor "truly stupid" and said poor kids should serve as janitors in their schools. He doesn't want to extend unemployment benefits, because, he says, "I'm opposed to giving people money for doing nothing."

Sumner, likewise, warned against handouts to people he termed "negligent, shiftless, inefficient, silly, and imprudent." Here's Sumner, more than a century ago: "Millionaires are a product of natural selection, acting on the whole body of men to pick out those who can meet the requirement of certain work to be done. . . . It is because they are thus selected that wealth—both their own and that entrusted to them—aggregates under their hands. . . . They may fairly be regarded as the naturally selected agents of society." Although they live in luxury, "the bargain is a good one for society."

Other Republican hopefuls also fit Sumner's mold. Ron Paul, who favored repeal of President Obama's health-care

plan, was asked at a Republican debate in September 2011 what medical response he'd recommend if a young man who had decided not to buy health insurance were to go into a coma. Paul's response:

"That's what freedom is all about: taking your own risks."
The Republican crowd cheered. If the young man died for
lack of health insurance, he was responsible. Survival of the
fittest.

Read the writings of the current darling of conservative intellectuals, the sociologist Charles Murray, and you
find the same philosophy at work. In his latest book, *Coming Apart,* Murray attributes the decline of the white working class to what he sees as their loss of traditional values
of diligence and hard work. Increasingly addicted to drugs,
failing to marry, giving birth out of wedlock, dropping out of
high school, and remaining jobless for long periods of time,
America's white working class has, in Murray's view, brought
its problems on itself. Government has aided and abetted
the decline by providing too much help in the form of social
programs that encourage pathologies and dependence.

Murray and other neo–social Darwinists seem not to
have noticed that for the past thirty years the old working
class's wages have declined, steady union jobs once available to them have disappeared, the economic base of their
communities has deteriorated, and their share of the nation's income and wealth has dramatically shrunk. It seems
more likely that these are the underlying sources of the social problems and pathologies Murray chronicles, but this
logic is inconvenient because it suggests that any solution
requires reversing the widening inequities that have hit the
old working class especially hard.

A hundred years ago social Darwinism offered a moral
justification for the wild inequities and social cruelties of the
late nineteenth century. It allowed John D. Rockefeller, for
example, to claim the fortune he accumulated through his

giant Standard Oil Trust was "merely a survival of the fittest." It was, he insisted, "the working out of a law of nature
and of God." The social Darwinism of that era also under-
mined all efforts to build a more broadly based prosperity
and rescue our democracy from the tight grip of a very few
at the top. It was used by the privileged and powerful to convince everyone else that government shouldn't do much of
anything.

Not until the twentieth century did America reject social
Darwinism. We created the large middle class that became
the engine of our economy and our democracy. We built
safety nets to catch Americans who fell downward, often
through no fault of their own. We designed regulations to
protect against the inevitable excesses of free-market greed.
We taxed the rich and invested in public goods—public
schools, public universities, public transportation, public
parks, public health—that made us all better off. In short,
we rejected the notion that each of us is on his or her own in
a competitive contest for survival.

Even the GOP eventually disavowed social Darwinism. Between the 1950s and 1970s, Republicans like Mark
Hatfield of Oregon, Jacob Javits and Nelson Rockefeller of
New York, Margaret Chase Smith of Maine, and Presidents
Dwight Eisenhower and Richard Nixon lent their support
to such interventionist measures as Medicare and the Environmental Protection Agency. Eisenhower pushed for the
greatest public works project in the history of the United
States, the National Interstate and Defense Highways Act,
which linked the nation together with four-lane (and occasionally six-lane) interstate highways covering forty thousand miles. The GOP also backed large expansion of feder-
ally supported higher education. And to many Republicans

at the time, a marginal income tax rate of more than 70 percent on top incomes was not repugnant.

The Republican Party of that era had its share of kooks and crackpots, such as Senator Joe McCarthy of Wisconsin, who conducted an infamous communist witch hunt, and General Douglas MacArthur, who told the Republican convention of 1952 that the Democratic Party had "become captive to the schemers and planners who have infiltrated its ranks of leadership to set the national course unerringly toward the socialistic regimentation of a totalitarian state." But for the most part, the party's elders controlled the nutcases.

Yet the Republican Party that emerged at the end of the twentieth century began to march backward to the nineteenth. Ronald Reagan lent his charm and single-mindedness to the movement, but he was not a true regressive. It was only when Newt Gingrich and his followers took over the House of Representatives in 1995 that regressives began retaking the GOP. The Koch brothers bankrolled the so-called Tea Party movement, and in 2010 Tea Party Republicans led the way toward capturing the House of Representatives and many state governments.

The Republican Party that emerged in 2012 is more radical and extreme than it's been in more than eighty years. Don't just take my word for it. Norman Ornstein, a distinguished political observer and resident scholar at the American Enterprise Institute, hardly a liberal bastion, and his colleague Thomas Mann of the Brookings Institution, another highly respected student of American politics, have been studying Washington politics and Congress for more than four decades. Over the years they've criticized both parties when they felt criticism was warranted. But in an

Op-Ed for the April 27, 2012, *Washington Post* they wrote that
they had never seen Washington so dysfunctional. "We have
no choice but to acknowledge that the core of the problem
lies with the Republican Party," which, in their words, has
become "ideologically extreme; scornful of compromise;
unmoved by conventional understanding of facts, evidence
and science; and dismissive of the legitimacy of its political
opposition." While the Democrats "may have moved from
their 40-yard line to their 25, the Republicans have gone
from their 40 to somewhere behind their goal post."

By 2012 the term "moderate Republican" had become
as much of an oxymoron as the term "liberal Republican"
was in the 1990s. Even conservative Republicans, such as
Senator Orrin Hatch of Utah, were targeted by the regressive right as being insufficiently orthodox and too willing to
compromise. During the battle over raising the debt ceiling that raged through the summer of 2011, the former Republican senator Chuck Hagel of Nebraska told the *Financial
Times* that his party had become "captive to political movements that are very ideological, that are very narrow. I've
never seen so much intolerance as I see today in American
politics." The veteran Republican congressional staffer Michael Lofgren wrote that "the Republican Party is becoming
less and less like a traditional political party in a representative democracy and becoming more like an apocalyptic cult,
or one of the intensely ideological authoritarian parties of
20th century Europe."

Through a sequence of presidential appointments, regressives have also gained a slim majority on the Supreme Court.

Antonin Scalia and Clarence Thomas, along with Samuel Alito, John Roberts, and, all too often, Anthony Kennedy, claim to be conservative jurists. But they have proven to be judicial activists bent on overturning seventy-five years of jurisprudence by resurrecting states' rights, treating the Second Amendment as if America still relied on local militias, narrowing the commerce clause, and, as I said earlier, calling corporations "people."

In 2010, Thomas and Scalia swung the Court in the direction of the right-wing group Citizens United, plaintiffs in the case that struck down federal laws limiting corporate campaign contributions. Before the decision, Thomas and Scalia had participated in a political retreat hosted by the billionaire financiers Charles and David Koch, driving forces behind loosening restrictions on big money in politics. Years before, when Thomas was nominated to the Supreme Court, Citizens United had spent $100,000 to support his nomination.

Given his connections with Citizens United and with the Koch brothers, Thomas should have recused himself from the *Citizens United* decision in order to avoid the appearance of a conflict of interest. He has also failed to disclose financial information about his wife's employment. Virginia Thomas is the founder of Liberty Central, a Tea Party organization now receiving unlimited corporate contributions due to *Citizens United*. Among the things she has lobbied for are the repeal of what she terms the "unconstitutional" health-care legislation.

Scalia isn't much better. In December 2011 he met in a closed-door session with Michele Bachmann's Tea Party Caucus, a group formed in large part to fight for the repeal of health-care reform. Can you imagine the firestorm if Justice Sonia Sotomayor met in secret with the Congressional Progressive Caucus?

I'm not so naive as to believe that Supreme Court justices don't have political views and values. But if the Court is perceived by the public to be politically partisan, it loses the public's confidence. That confidence, as described by Justice Stephen Breyer in his impassioned dissent in *Bush v. Gore* (a case like *Citizens United* that could be understood only in partisan political terms), "is a public treasure. It has been built slowly over many years" and is a "vitally necessary ingredient of any successful effort to protect basic liberty and, indeed, the rule of law itself." When Clarence Thomas and Antonin Scalia go to political strategy sessions with Republican partisans, they jeopardize everything the Supreme Court stands for.

Regressives have no new ideas for dealing with any challenge of the twenty-first century. Which of the 2012 GOP presidential aspirants do you think delivered the following words at the most recent Conservative Political Action Conference?

> We have seen tax-and-tax, spend-and-spend reach a fantastic total greater than in all the previous . . . years of our Republic. . . . Behind this plush curtain of tax and spend, three sinister spooks or ghosts are mixing poison for the American people. They are the shades of Mussolini, with his bureaucratic fascism; of Karl Marx, and his socialism; and of Lord Keynes, with his perpetual government spending, deficits, and inflation. And we added a new ideology of our own.

> That is government give-away programs. . . . If
> you want to see pure socialism mixed with give-
> away programs, take a look at socialized medicine.

If you guessed Newt Gingrich, you could be forgiven;
he didn't utter these precise words, although he uses much
the same language and offers the same themes. You'd also
be wrong if you guessed Mitt Romney or Rick Santorum,
Rick Perry, Sarah Palin, or Ron Paul. But again your mistake
would be understandable, because any of them could have
delivered this message, and all of them have delivered varia-
tions of it, over and over. So have Republican candidates for
seats in Congress, state legislatures and governorships, and
local elections. It's the Republican message of 2012 and beyond.

The correct answer, however, is Herbert Hoover.

Hoover didn't deliver these words at the last Conservative Political Action Conference. He delivered them at the
Republican National Convention in Chicago on July 8,
1952. My point is regressives haven't come up with a single
new idea since, or a new theme. It would be one thing if
Hoover was always correct. But, as you may remember, the
former president did not have a sterling record when it came
to the economy. As president, he presided over the crash of
1929 and ushered in the Great Depression. He had no idea
how to respond. By the time he was voted out of office in
1932, one of four Americans was unemployed.

By 1952, Hoover was hidebound and irrelevant. After
Dwight D. Eisenhower won the 1952 Republican nomina-
tion and went on to become president, he wisely disregarded
everything Hoover had advised. Under Ike, the marginal
income tax on America's highest earners was raised to 91

percent. As I've said, Eisenhower also commenced the biggest infrastructure program in the nation's history—the National Interstate and Defense Highways Act. He also expanded Social Security and signed into law the National Defense Education Act, which trained a whole generation of math and science teachers and upgraded American classrooms for the future. Under Ike, the Defense Department spawned technologies that would cement America's leadership in aerospace and telecommunications for more than a generation.

The United States did not suffer fascism, socialism, deficits, and inflation, as Hoover predicted. Instead, the U.S. economy roared. The median wage rose faster than ever before, and the incomes of America's working class and poor rose at the fastest pace of all. Our democracy became sufficiently confident and expansive that within a few years we passed the historic Civil Rights Act of 1964 and the Voting Rights Act of 1965.

THE STOP-AT-NOTHING TACTIC

Social Darwinism is the regressives' theme. Stop at nothing is their methodology. As the political analyst Michael Lind has noted, today's Tea Party is less an ideological movement than the latest incarnation of an angry white minority—

predominantly southern and mainly rural—that has repeatedly attacked American democracy in order to get its way. It's
no mere coincidence that the states responsible for putting
the most Tea Party representatives in the House are all former members of the Confederacy. Of Congress's Tea Party
Caucus elected in 2010, twelve members hailed from Texas,
seven from Florida, five from Louisiana, five from Georgia,
and three each from South Carolina, Tennessee, and the
border state Missouri. Others were from border states with
significant southern populations and southern ties. The four
Californians in the caucus were from the inland part of the
state or Orange County, whose political culture was shaped
by Oklahomans and southerners who migrated there during
the Great Depression. This isn't to say all Tea Partiers are
white, southern, or rural Republicans—only that these char-
acteristics define the epicenter of Tea Party Land.

The views separating these primarily white, southern,
and rural Republicans from other Republicans mirror the
split between self-described Tea Partiers and what had been
the Republican establishment. In a poll of Republicans conducted for CNN in September 2011, nearly six in ten who
identified themselves with the Tea Party said global warm-
ing isn't a proven fact; other Republicans said it is. Six in ten
Tea Partiers said evolution is wrong; other Republicans were
split on the issue. Tea Party Republicans are twice as likely
as other Republicans to say abortion should be illegal in all
circumstances, and half as likely to support gay marriage. Tea
Party Republicans are more vehement advocates of states'
rights than other Republicans. Six in ten Tea Partiers want
to abolish the Department of Education; only one in five
other Republicans do. And Tea Party Republicans worry
more about the federal deficit than about jobs, while other

Republicans say reducing unemployment is more important than reducing the deficit.

In other words, the regressives who are taking over the GOP aren't that much different from the social conservatives who began asserting themselves in the party during the 1990s and, before them, the "Willie Horton" conservatives of the 1980s and, before them, Richard Nixon's so-called "silent majority." Through most of those years, though, the GOP managed to contain these white, mainly rural, and mostly southern radicals. For one thing, many of them were still Democrats. The conservative mantle of the GOP remained in the West and the Midwest—with the libertarian legacies of the Ohio senator Robert A. Taft and Barry Goldwater, neither of whom was a barn burner—while the center of the party remained in New York and the East, safely within the corporate establishment and Wall Street.

But after the Civil Rights Act of 1964, as the South began its long march toward the Republican Party and New York and the East became ever more solidly Democratic, it was only a matter of time. The GOP's dominant coalition of big business, Wall Street, and midwestern and western libertarians was losing its grip.

The watershed event was Gingrich's takeover of the House in 1995. Suddenly, it seemed, the GOP had a personality transplant. The gentlemanly conservatism of the Republican House minority leader Bob Michel was replaced by the bomb-throwing antics of Gingrich, Dick Armey, and Tom DeLay. Almost overnight Washington was transformed from a place where legislators sought common ground into a war zone. Compromise was replaced by brinksmanship, bargaining by obstructionism, normal legislative maneuvering by threats to close down government—which occurred at the end of 1995.

Before then, when I'd testified on the Hill as secretary of labor, I had come in for tough questioning from Republican senators and representatives—which was their job. After January 1995, I was verbally assaulted. "Mr. Secretary, are you a socialist?" I recall one of them asking. The new crowd wasn't willing to compromise on anything. Their distinguishing characteristic was that they'd stop at nothing to get their way. Led by Gingrich, House Republicans closed down the government when they didn't get their way on the budget. Then stop-at-nothing regressives voted to impeach Bill Clinton. In the upper house, two-thirds of senators from the South voted for impeachment. (A majority of the Senate, you may recall, voted to acquit.)

According to Norman Ornstein and Thomas Mann, the two respected political observers I mentioned before, Gingrich was instrumental in the GOP's move to the extreme right. "From the day he entered Congress in 1979," they write, "Mr. Gingrich had a strategy to create a Republican majority in the House: convincing voters that the institution was so corrupt that anyone would be better than the incumbents, especially those in the Democratic majority." It took Gingrich sixteen years, but by bringing ethics charges against Democratic leaders, exploiting scandals to create even more public disgust with politicians, and recruiting right-wing GOP candidates around the country to run against Washington, he eventually accomplished his goal. "The forces Mr. Gingrich unleashed destroyed whatever comity existed across party lines," say Ornstein and Mann, "activated an extreme and virulently anti-Washington base—most recently represented by Tea Party activists—and helped drive moderate Republicans out of Congress."

America has had a long history of white southern radicals who would stop at nothing to get their way—seceding from the Union in 1861, repudiating federal laws designed to protect the rights of black citizens during Reconstruction, enacting Jim Crow laws, resisting desegregation orders in the 1950s, and refusing to obey civil rights legislation in the 1960s. The Gingrich-led government shutdown at the end of 1995 was a prelude to the 2011 showdown over raising the federal debt ceiling—which could have triggered a government default and risked the full faith and credit of the United States. Gingrich's recent assertion during the Republican primaries that public officials aren't bound to follow the decisions of federal courts is in the same tradition.

The GOP's stop-at-nothing insurgents hate government more than they hate the national debt. They refuse to reduce that debt with tax increases, even with tax increases on the wealthy, because a tax increase doesn't reduce the size of government. By contrast, what's left of the Republican establishment—still occasionally found on Wall Street and in corporate suites—dislikes the national debt more than it dislikes government, and it opposes using the threat of a default as a bargaining chip. It doesn't want America's creditors to become spooked about the risk of runaway inflation or a future default, because it depends on smooth-functioning credit markets and a stable dollar.

Some Americans tolerate the stop-at-nothing assault on our system of government because they're searching for a villain to blame for their continuing economic fears and insecurities, and government is a convenient scapegoat. At the same time, most of what government does that helps them is now so deeply woven into the thread of daily life that it's no longer recognizable as government. Think of the indignant Republican voters who showed up at congressional town-hall meetings to protest President Obama's health-care bill shouting, "Don't take away my Medicare!" The Cornell political scientist Suzanne Mettler found that more than 44 percent of Social Security recipients say they "have not used a government social program," as do more than half of families receiving government-backed student loans, 43 percent of unemployment insurance beneficiaries, and almost 30 percent of recipients of Social Security disability. Add in the relentless government hating and baiting of Fox News and Rush Limbaugh and his imitators on rage radio; include more than thirty years of Ronald Reagan's repeated refrain that government is the problem; pile on hundreds of millions of dollars from regressive billionaires like Charles and David Koch, intent on convincing the public that government is evil, and some public support for stop-at-nothing tactics is not all that surprising.

Yet neither the regressives' stop-at-nothing tactics nor their social Darwinist message would have gained much traction were it not for the stunning failure of Democrats to make the case for a strong and effective government that responds to the needs of average people. There is no shortage of evidence—globalizing corporations, rip-roaring CEO pay, mass layoffs, declining pay for the bottom 90 percent, mine disasters, exploding oil rigs, malfeasance on Wall Street, and wildly escalating costs of health insurance—and it is not especially difficult to connect the dots. Yet too frequently Democrats have appeared timid and defensive; too often they've given in to regressive demands without a fight; and they've allowed the regressives' big lies to go unrebutted for too long.

Turning Morality Upside Down

A third method regressives have used to distort public understanding of what's at stake is to turn morality upside down. They vigorously condemn gay marriage, abortion, out-of-wedlock births, access to contraception, and the wall separating church and state.

In May 2012, North Carolina voters approved a Republican-proposed amendment to the state constitution banning same-sex marriage, joining twenty-nine other states with similar measures. Mitt Romney, the GOP presidential candidate, said he opposed same-sex marriage even as President Obama said he supported it. Meanwhile, Republicans introduced more than four hundred bills in state legislatures aimed at limiting womens' reproductive rights—banning abortions, requiring women seeking abortions to have invasive ultrasound tests beforehand, and limiting the use of contraceptives.

But America isn't suffering a breakdown in private morality. It's burdened by a breakdown in public morality. What Americans do in their bedrooms is their own business. What corporate executives and Wall Street financiers do in boardrooms and executive suites affects all of us. We're not in trouble because gays want to marry or women want to have some control over when they have babies. We're in trouble because CEOs are collecting exorbitant pay while slicing the pay of average workers, because the titans of Wall

Street demand short-term results over long-term jobs, and because of a boardroom culture that tolerates financial conflicts of interest, insider trading, and the outright bribery of public officials through unlimited campaign "donations."

What's truly immoral is not what adults choose to do with other consenting adults but what those with great power have chosen to do to the rest of us. America's problems have nothing to do with private morality. The breakdown is in public morality—abuses of public trust that undermine the integrity of our economy and democracy and have led millions of Americans to conclude the game is fixed.

Yet the regressive bedroom crowd doesn't want to talk about the nation's boardrooms, because that's where most of their campaign money comes from. They'd rather use bedroom morality as another means of distracting voters from what's really going on. Regressives have no problem intrud-

ing on the most personal and most intimate decisions people make while railing against government intrusions on big
business. They don't hesitate to hurl the epithets "shame-
ful," "disgraceful," and "contemptible" at private moral decisions they disagree with while staying stone silent in the face
of the most contemptible violations of public trust at the
highest reaches of the economy.

The late political scientist James Q. Wilson noted that
a broken window left unattended signals that no one cares
if windows are broken. It becomes an ongoing invitation
to throw more stones at more windows, ultimately undermining moral standards of the entire community. Apply
that logic to America and you'll find that the windows Wall
Street broke in the years leading up to the crash of 2008 remain broken. In fact, these sorts of windows began shatter-
ing years ago. Enron's court-appointed trustee reported that
bankers from Citigroup and JPMorgan Chase didn't merely
look the other way; they dreamed up and sold Enron financial schemes specifically designed to allow Enron to commit
fraud. Arthur Andersen, Enron's auditor, was convicted of
obstructing justice by shredding Enron documents, yet most
of the Andersen partners who aided and abetted Enron
were never punished.

Americans are entitled to their own religious views about
gay marriage, contraception, out-of-wedlock births, abortion, and God. We can be truly free only if we're confident
we can go about our private lives without being monitored
or intruded upon by government and can practice whatever
faith (or lack of faith) we wish regardless of the religious
beliefs of others. A society where one set of religious views
is imposed on a large number of citizens who disagree with
them is not a democracy. It's a theocracy.

Yet an economy is built on a foundation of shared *public* morality. Adam Smith, the putative founder of modern economics, never called himself an economist. The separate field of economics didn't exist in the eighteenth century, when Smith wrote. He called himself a moral philosopher. And the book he was proudest of wasn't *The Wealth of Nations* but his *Theory of Moral Sentiments*—about the ties that bind people together into societies. Those ties are now being shredded in America by the regressives. Rather than stop the abuses of economic power and privilege that are characterizing so many decisions in the nation's boardrooms and executive suites, they would rather stir up Americans about the most intimate decisions people make.

Regressives have turned morality upside down—and they've done it on purpose. It's just another way to divert the nation's attention and to divide us from one another.

THE REGRESSIVE STRATEGY: DIVIDE AND CONQUER

When they're not spouting social Darwinism, deploying stop-at-nothing tactics, or turning morality upside down, regressives have been trying to convince Americans we can no longer afford to do what we need to do as a nation. They say America is broke. So the only way any of us can get by in the future—keep our jobs, make our families economically secure, have enough money for retirement, preserve the public services and safety nets we rely on—is by forcing other middle- or lower-income Americans to give up even more.

The regressive aim is to divide and conquer: as I said, to pit unionized workers against non-unionized, public sector workers against nonpublic, native-born Americans against immigrants—but also to set older workers within sight of Medicare and Social Security against younger workers who don't believe these programs will be there for them, the middle class against the poor, even religious conservatives against secularists.

It's another means of distracting attention from the extraordinary accumulation of income, wealth, and power at the very top and the historically low tax rates paid by the rich. And they hope no one notices their push for additional tax cuts for the rich—making the Bush tax cuts permanent, further reducing taxes on the rich, eliminating the estate tax, and allowing the wealthy to shift ever more of their income into capital gains, taxed at 15 percent.

Their divide-and-conquer strategy has three parts.

The first is being played out in the budget battles in Washington. By raising the alarm over deficit spending and simultaneously squeezing popular middle-class programs, regressives want the American public to view what happens in Washington as a giant zero-sum contest that some average Americans can win only if other average Americans lose. President Obama fell into the trap by calling for cuts in Medicare, along with other cuts in programs the poor and the working class depend on, such as assistance with home heating, community services, and college loans.

The second part of the divide-and-conquer strategy is being played out in the states, where public employees are being blamed for state budget crises. Unions didn't cause these crises—state revenues plummeted because of the Great Recession—but regressives view them as opportunities to gut public employee unions, starting with teachers. Governor Scott Walker of Wisconsin told a wealthy sup-

porter (who later contributed more than half a million dollars to help him fight off a recall) that his first step for reducing union power was "to deal with collective bargaining for all public employee unions because you divide and conquer." Soon thereafter, Walker and his GOP majority in the state legislature ended most union rights for public employees. Ohio's Republican governor, John Kasich, tried to push a similar plan through a Republican-dominated legislature there. New Jersey's governor, Chris Christie, attempted the same, telling a conservative conference, "I'm attacking the leadership of the union because they're greedy, and they're selfish and they're self-interested."

As I've noted, public employees don't earn more than their private sector counterparts when you take account of their education. In fact, over the last fifteen years the pay of public sector workers, including teachers, has dropped relative to private sector employees with the same level of education. Moreover, most public employees don't have generous pensions. After a career with annual pay averaging less than $45,000, the typical newly retired public employee receives a pension of $19,000 a year. Yet regressives would rather go after teachers and other public employees than have us look at the pay of Wall Street traders, private-equity managers, and heads of hedge funds whose lending and investing practices were the proximate cause of the Great Recession to begin with and who owe their jobs to the giant taxpayer-supported bailout.

The third part of the divide-and-conquer strategy is being played out in the Supreme Court, which has been politicized more than at any time in recent memory. On January 21, 2010, as I noted earlier, a majority of the justices ruled that corporations have a right under the First Amendment to provide unlimited amounts of money to political candidates. *Citizens United v. Federal Election Commission* is among the most politically motivated and legally grotesque decisions of our highest court—ranking right up there with *Dred Scott v. Sandford.* Two months after the *Citizens United* decision, the U.S. Court of Appeals for the District of Columbia Circuit, relying on *Citizens United,* ruled that the existing $5,000-per-year limit on the amount any individual can contribute to a super PAC or other independent group also violates the First Amendment.

These three aspects of divide and conquer—a federal budget battle to shrink government focused on programs the vast middle class depends on; state efforts to undermine public employees whom the middle class depends on; and a Supreme Court dedicated to bending the Constitution to enlarge and entrench the political power of the wealthy—fit perfectly and diabolically together. They pit average working Americans against one another, distract attention from the almost unprecedented concentration of wealth and power at the top, and conceal regressive plans to further enlarge and entrench that wealth and power.

THE TEN BIGGEST ECONOMIC LIES

A final aspect of the regressive strategy is to tell a few big lies about the economy over and over. You hear them repeated endlessly on right-wing radio and on Fox News, and you read them incessantly on the editorial pages of *The Wall Street Journal*. Together they paint a picture of an America in which social Darwinism replaces the public good. Demagogues throughout history have known that big lies, repeated often enough, start being believed—unless they're rebutted. George Orwell once explained that when a public is stressed and confused, a big lie told repeatedly and unchallenged can become accepted truth. Make sure you know the facts and spread them.

The lies:

1. The rich are "job creators," so tax cuts for the rich trickle down to everyone else while higher taxes on the rich hurt the economy and slow job growth. Untrue. Look at recent history. George W. Bush cut taxes on the rich, and what happened? A fraction of the number of jobs were created under Bush than had been created under Bill Clinton, and the median wage dropped, adjusted for inflation. Trickle-down economics is a cruel joke.

As I've said, from the end of World War II until 1981, the richest Americans faced a top marginal tax rate of 70 percent or above. Under Dwight Eisenhower it was 91 percent. Even after all deductions and credits, the top taxes on the very rich were more than 52 percent—far higher than they've been since. Yet the economy grew faster during those years than it has since. During almost three decades spanning 1951 to 1980, when the top rate was between 70 percent and 91 percent, average annual growth in the American economy was 3.7 percent. Between 1983 and the start of the Great Recession, when the top rate dropped to between 35 percent and 39 percent, average growth was 3 percent.

Regressives say small businesses would be hurt by a higher marginal tax. Don't believe this, either. Only just over 1 percent of small-business owners earn enough to be taxed at the top rate—and that's just on the portion of their incomes exceeding $379,000.

The rich don't create jobs. Jobs are created when the vast majority of Americans buy enough to make companies add capacity and hire more workers. But that won't happen unless the vast majority has enough money to do the buying. As I've said, when a disproportionate amount of national income goes to the rich, the middle class no longer has the purchasing power to create these additional jobs.

2. *American corporations would create more jobs and spur the economy forward if their taxes were lower.* Wrong again. American corporations don't need tax cuts. As I've noted, many of them, like General Electric, manipulate the tax code so they don't pay any taxes at all. Besides, large and middle-sized companies are having no difficulty getting loans at bargain-basement rates, courtesy of the Fed. Big companies are sitting on more than $2 trillion of cash right now that they don't know what to do with.

The reason they're not investing in additional capacity or many new jobs has nothing to do with taxes. It's that they don't see enough customers with enough money in their pockets to buy what the additional capacity would produce.

Businesses are spending as much as they can justify economically. Almost two-thirds of the measly growth in the economy in 2011 came from businesses rebuilding their inventories. But without more consumer spending, businesses won't spend more. A robust economy can't be built on inventory replacements.

The wrongheaded idea that corporations need tax cuts to create jobs is also being used by regressive governors who are cutting business taxes willy-nilly in order to compete with other states that are doing the same. They've entered into a giant zero-sum game that doesn't create a single new job overall but robs the states of money needed for critical investments in schools and infrastructure. In 2012, Florida's governor, Rick Scott, said his corporate tax cuts "will give Florida a competitive edge in attracting jobs." But Florida simultaneously cut education spending by $3 billion, when the state already ranked near the bottom in per-pupil spending and had one of the nation's lowest graduation rates. Even if Scott's tax cuts created jobs, the jobs would pay peanuts.

3. We'd have more jobs and a better economy if we shrank the size of government. Wrong. Shrinking government results in fewer government workers—including teachers, firefighters, police officers, and social workers at the state and local levels, and safety inspectors and military personnel at the federal level. And it results in fewer government contractors who therefore employ fewer private sector workers. This is the same claptrap regressives have been mouthing for decades. Their ultimate goal, in the words of the regressive guru Grover Norquist, is to take government "down to the size where we can drown it in the bathtub."

I recently debated a conservative Republican who insisted the best way to revive the American economy was to shrink government. When I asked him to explain his logic, he said, simply, "Government is the source of all our problems." When I noted government spending had brought the economy out of the Great Depression, he disagreed. "The Depression ended because of World War II," he pronounced, as if government had played no part in World War II.

4. *We'd have a stronger economy if we had fewer regulations.* Untrue. As I said before, corporations exist for one reason only—to make a profit and thereby increase the value of their shares, not to protect the public. Yet public health and safety, fairness to small investors, and a sustainable environment are all public goods. Without them, we'd be the poorer for it. Regulations make sense where the benefits to the public exceed the costs, and regulations should be designed to maximize those benefits and minimize those costs. Period.

5. *The economy would improve if we cut the budget deficit right now.* Baloney. As long as many Americans are still out of work, the first priority must be jobs and growth. Government spending counteracts the shortfall in private spending. Until employment and growth are restored to normal levels, budget cuts only increase unemployment and reduce tax revenues. We should start cutting the federal budget only when the economy is back on track, when unemployment drops to around 5 percent and growth is back to 3 percent.

Don't get me wrong. The national debt is a problem, but the ratio of debt owed by the government to the economy's total output of goods and services in 2012 wasn't nearly as high as it was after World War II—when it reached 120 percent. If we move more quickly toward a full recovery, the debt-to-GDP ratio will fall, as it did in the 1950s. Revenues will flow into the Treasury, and much of the current "budget crisis" will evaporate. Growth and jobs are the key. When more people are working, more companies are profiting, the economy is expanding, revenues pour into national treasuries, and the debt declines relative to the economy.

When the economy grows more slowly or contracts, the opposite occurs. Economies can fall into vicious cycles of slower growth and lower tax revenues. If governments then cut public spending, the vicious cycle can become an austerity death trap. The debt-to-GDP ratio worsens because the economy shrinks even faster. Much of Europe fell into that trap in 2012. Output shrank after Britain and the euro zone adopted austerity measures and slashed public budgets in an attempt to gain control over public debts. If regressives have their way, America will join Europe.

It comes down to a question of timing. If government slices spending too early, when unemployment is high and growth is slowing, the debt situation worsens. That's because public spending is a critical component of total demand. If demand is already lagging, spending cuts further slow the economy—and thereby increase the size of the government debt relative to the size of the overall economy. We'd end up with the worst of both worlds—a growing ratio of debt to the gross domestic product, coupled with high unemployment and a public that's furious about losing safety nets when they're most needed. The proper sequence is for government to keep spending until jobs and growth are restored, and only then to take out the budget ax.

The Fed can't possibly generate a buoyant recovery on its own. Without an expansionary fiscal policy, the Fed's low interest rates have little effect. Companies won't borrow in order to expand and hire more workers unless they're confident they will have customers for what they produce. And consumers won't borrow money to spend on goods and services unless they're confident they'll have jobs.

The 2011 downgrade of America's debt by Standard & Poor's (S&P) is irrelevant. S&P downgraded the debt because Congress and the president didn't reach a long-term debt agreement to S&P's liking. Pardon me for asking, but who gave S&P the authority to tell America how much debt it has to shed, and how? If we pay our bills, we're a good credit risk. If we don't, or aren't likely to, we're a bad credit risk. And because most of our bills are denominated in dollars, which we print, it's highly likely we can pay. When, how, and by how much we bring down the long-term debt—or, more accurately, the ratio of debt to GDP—is none of S&P's business. S&P's intrusion into American politics is also ironic because much of our current debt is directly or indirectly due to S&P's failure (along with the failures of the two other major credit-rating agencies, Fitch and Moody's) to do its job before the financial meltdown. Until the eve of the collapse, S&P gave triple-A ratings to some of the Street's riskiest packages of mortgage-backed securities and collateralized debt obligations. Had S&P fulfilled its responsibility and warned investors of how much risk Wall Street was taking on, the housing and debt bubbles wouldn't have become so large, and their bursts wouldn't have brought down much of the economy. You and I and other taxpayers wouldn't have had to bail out Wall Street; millions of Americans would have spent the subsequent years working instead of collecting unemployment insurance; the government wouldn't have had to inject the economy with a massive stimulus to save millions of other jobs; and far more tax revenue would have been pouring into the Treasury from individuals and businesses.

One final point you should know about the federal budget: the mammoth deficits that will be racked up beyond 2020 are due almost entirely to rapidly rising health-care costs along with seventy-seven million baby boomers whose bodies will slowly be deteriorating. At the rate health-care costs are already rising, they'll also drive average American families into ruin. Which raises the next regressive falsehood . . .

6. *Medicare and Medicaid have to be scaled back.* Untrue. The reason their costs are rising so fast is that the nation's overall health-care costs are rising so fast. A related lie: *The way to slow the growth of Medicare is to give seniors vouchers that can be cashed in for private insurance.* That's the regressives' plan that most House Republicans voted for in 2012—and it's dead wrong. Any budget savings would come directly out of the pockets of seniors, as the vouchers fall further and further behind the rising costs of health care. The inevitable result would be that more and more seniors would be priced out of the market for health care as the underlying costs of health care continue to soar. A far better way to slow medical costs is to use Medicare and Medicaid's bargaining power over drug companies and hospitals to get lower prices and to move from a fee-for-service system to a fee-for-healthy-outcomes system. And because Medicare has far lower administrative costs than private health insurers, we should make Medicare available to everyone. I'll get to this in more detail a bit later.

7. *Our safety nets are overly generous.* To repeat: In Mitt Romney's standard stump speech during the 2012 campaign, he charged President Obama with creating a nation of dependents: "Over the past three years Barack Obama has been replacing our merit-based society with an entitlement society." During the Republican primary, Rick Santorum said,

"There's a push to get more and more people dependent." Newt Gingrich called Obama "the best food-stamp president in American history."

What was their evidence? They pointed to federal budget data showing that direct payments to individuals shot up by almost $600 billion, a 32 percent increase, from the start of 2009 to 2012. They also referred to census data showing that by 2012, 49 percent of Americans lived in homes where at least one person was collecting a federal benefit—Social Security, food stamps, unemployment insurance, workers' compensation, or subsidized housing. That was up from 44 percent in 2008. And they trumpeted Social Security Administration figures showing that the number of people on Social Security disability jumped 10 percent during Obama's first two years in office. From this evidence they argued our economic problems stem from this sharp rise in "dependency." Get rid of these benefits and people will work harder.

But again they have cause and effect backward. The reason for the rise in food stamps, unemployment insurance, and other safety net programs was that Americans got clobbered in 2008 with the worst economic catastrophe since the Great Depression. They and their families needed whatever helping hands they could get.

If anything, America's safety nets have been too small and shot through with holes. That's why the number and percentage of Americans in poverty increased dramatically between 2009 and 2012. This is the real scandal. For example, at the height of the recession only 40 percent of the unemployed qualified for unemployment benefits because they weren't working full-time or long enough on a single job before they were let go. The unemployment system doesn't take account of the fact that a large portion of the workforce

typically works part-
time on several jobs
and moves from
job to job. By 2012,
although much of
the nation was still
suffering the after-
effects of recession,
only a small portion

of the poor qualified for welfare. This was because the 1996
legislation that formally ended the old Aid to Families with
Dependent Children program provided just five years of
aid in a person's lifetime. Given the prolonged recession, by
2012 many poor Americans had reached their lifetime limit.

Republicans also promised to repeal President Obama's
health-care law, which covers thirty million more Americans than were covered before. That law still left more than
twenty million without health insurance. They and any others who would lose medical coverage if the new law were
repealed will get emergency care when they're in dire straits
in any event—hospitals won't refuse them—but we all end
up paying indirectly.

Regressives pretend they're about opportunity. But in reality, as I've said before, they're promoting social Darwinism.

8. Social Security is a Ponzi scheme. Don't believe it. In a former life I was a trustee of the Social Security trust fund, and
I know how the Social Security actuaries make their pro-
jections. Social Security is solvent for the next twenty-five
years, until 2037. It could be solvent for the next century if
we raised the ceiling on income subject to the Social Security payroll tax. As I write, that ceiling is $110,100.

Until 2010, Social Security took in more payroll taxes

than it paid out in benefits. It lent the surpluses to the rest of the government. Now that Social Security has started to pay out more than it takes in, the trust fund, by law, is entitled to collect what the rest of the government owes it. This will keep it fully solvent for those twenty-five years. The only reason there will be a problem after that point concerns a mistake made in 1983, when Alan Greenspan's National Commission on Social Security Reform was supposed to have fixed the system for good. Congress accepted the Greenspan Commission's recommendations to gradually increase payroll taxes and raise the retirement age (early boomers like me can start collecting full benefits at age sixty-six; late boomers born after 1960 will have to wait until they're sixty-seven). But the Greenspan Commission failed to take account of widening inequality. In fairness, inequality was just beginning to widen at that point, so the error was understandable.

Bear with me for a moment, because it's important you understand what happened then. The Social Security payroll tax applies only to earnings up to a certain ceiling, which rises annually according to a formula roughly matching inflation. In 1983, the ceiling was set so the Social Security payroll tax would apply to 90 percent of all wages covered by Social Security, and that 90 percent figure was built into the Greenspan Commission's fixes. Today, though, the Social Security payroll tax affects only about 84 percent of total income. It went from 90 percent to 84 percent because a larger and larger portion of total income has gone to the top.

So the logical response to Social Security's long-term problem is to raise the ceiling on income subject to the Social Security tax, rather than to reduce benefits or raise the age of eligibility.

9. *It's unfair that middle- and lower-income Americans have been pay-ing a smaller share of federal income taxes and some pay no income tax at all.* There's nothing unfair about it. Fairness requires that people who make more money pay a higher portion of their incomes in taxes than people with less money. That's called a progressive tax system, and it's been a foundation stone of America's tax code. Because the share of total income going to the top 1 percent has doubled since the late 1970s, we'd expect their share of total taxes to have doubled as well, and the share paid by middle- and lower-income Americans to have dropped. In fact, the top 1 percent's share of total taxes has not kept pace with their increasing share of total income. If the tax system were totally fair, their share of tax revenues would be more, and everyone else's share would be less.

Besides, the income tax is only one of the taxes Americans pay. Middle- and lower-income Americans are now paying a significantly larger share of their incomes than are wealthy Americans in payroll taxes (Social Security and Medicare), state and local sales taxes, user fees, and property taxes. Data from the Institute on Taxation and Economic Policy show that the poorest fifth of households paid 12.3 percent of their incomes in state and local taxes in 2010. When all fed-eral, state, and local taxes are taken into account, the bottom fifth paid a stunning 16.3 percent of their incomes in taxes, on average, a larger percentage than Mitt Romney paid in federal taxes on his $21 million of income that year.

10. *A flat tax would be fairer.* Don't believe it. All flat-tax pro-posals benefit the rich more than the poor for one simple reason: today's tax code is still at least moderately progres-sive. The rich usually pay a higher percentage of their in-comes in income taxes than do the poor. A flat tax would eliminate that slight progressivity.

Flat taxers pretend a flat tax is good public policy, for two reasons. First, they say, it would simplify paying taxes. Baloney. Flat-tax proposals don't eliminate all deductions. In every plan I've seen, people with families will still be able to deduct their dependents, while single people will pay a higher rate, businesses will deduct their expenses, and in most plans people with homes will still be able to deduct interest on their mortgages. All this means most taxpayers would still have lots of paperwork.

Second, proponents of a flat tax say it's fairer than the current system because a flat tax "treats everyone the same." The truth is that in the current tax code, everyone whose income reaches the same bracket is treated the same as everyone else whose income reaches that bracket (apart from various deductions, exemptions, and credits, of course). For example, no one pays any income taxes on the first $20,000 or so of his income. People in higher brackets pay a higher rate only on the portion of their income that hits that bracket—not on their entire incomes. Regressive Republicans have tried to sow confusion about this. They want Americans to believe, for example, that if the Bush tax cuts ended, small-business owners with incomes of $251,000 a year would have to pay 39 percent of their entire incomes in taxes rather than 35 percent. Wrong. They'd only have to pay the 39 percent rate on $1,000—the portion of their incomes over $250,000.

Get it? We already have a flat tax—flat within each bracket. The real problem is the top brackets are set too low relative to where the money is. The topmost bracket starts at $388,350 on income earned in 2012. People with incomes higher than that pay 35 percent—again, only on that portion of their incomes exceeding $388,350. This means a doctor who's making, say, $390,000 a year pays the same income tax rate as a plutocrat pulling in $2 billion or $20 billion. Regressives are pushing the flat tax as a smoke screen. They'd rather not have anyone talk about the unfairness and fiscal absurdity of the current system.

These ten whoppers have been repeated so often by regressives and their media outlets that many Americans have started to believe them. But every one of them is a lie. Yet regressives won't debate their lies because they know they can't win if they do. That's why they typically use ad hominem accusation in place of argument. In April 2012, Representative Alan West, a Florida Republican, asserted there were "78 to 81" Democrats in Congress who are members of the Communist Party. What made West's charge particularly disturbing was that not a single Republican member of Congress, presidential candidate, or any other Republican leader condemned it. Apparently such extremist rhetoric is now taken for granted. Even I've been on the receiving end. Bill O'Reilly, the tumescent personality of Fox News, said on his show, "Robert Reich is a communist who secretly adores Karl Marx."

West's and O'Reilly's accusations were odd, to say the least. It's hard to find a communist anywhere these days (for the record, I'm not one). O'Reilly's charge wasn't even logical. How could he know if I "secretly" adore Karl Marx, if it's a secret? (I don't secretly adore Karl Marx.) Ordinarily I

don't bother repeating anything Bill O'Reilly says but
this particular whopper is
significant because it repre-
sents what O'Reilly and Fox
News, among other mega-
phones of the regressive
right, are doing to the national dialogue—burying it under
vitriol. O'Reilly based his claim on an interview I did with
Jon Stewart on *The Daily Show* in which I pointed out that
because America's big corporations are now global we can
no longer rely on them to make the investments in human
capital or basic research that America needs, so government
has to step in. But O'Reilly had no interest in arguing the
point. Although I asked repeatedly, he refused to debate me.

Ad hominem attacks are always the last refuges of those
lacking logic or facts. But such attacks are becoming a sub-
stitute for real debate in America. It's not that the nation
is more polarized than it's been in the past. The nation has
been through searing conflicts, some within the living mem-
ories of most of us. The communist witch hunts of the 1950s
were followed by the civil rights movement, the Vietnam
War, battles over womens' reproductive rights and gay marriage. What makes America's current polarization remarkable isn't the severity of our disagreements but the regressive
right's unwillingness to seriously debate them.

So many Americans are angry and frustrated these days—
vulnerable to loss of job and health care and home, without
a shred of economic security—they're easy prey for demagogues offering big lies. Yet the only antidote for big lies
is big truth—told relentlessly and powerfully. You must be
armed with it.

Part Three

Beyond Outrage:
What You Need to Do

Someone recently approached me at the cheese counter of a local supermarket, asking, "What can I do?" At first I thought the person was seeking advice about a choice of cheese. But I soon realized the question was larger than that. It was: What can I do about what's happening to America—an economic game increasingly rigged in favor of those at the top and against ordinary Americans, and a government that no longer seems to work for average people but is increasingly responsive to big money? In this part of the book I want to try to answer that question.

How to Make a Movement

I don't know where the Occupier movement is heading, but I do know there's great energy at America's grass roots for progressive change—more energy now than I've seen in de-

cades. The question is how to harness that energy and turn
it into a sustainable and powerful progressive movement to
take back our economy and our democracy from the regressive forces that have been gaining ground.

People who voted for Barack Obama in 2008 tended to
fall into one of two camps once he became president: trust-
ers, who believed he was a good man with the right values
and that as president did everything he could to put those
values into effect; and cynics, who became disillusioned with
his bailout of Wall Street, his flimsy plan to tame the Street,
his willingness to jettison the "public option" in his health-
care plan, and his negotiating strategy that always seems to
begin by giving away the store.

In my view, both positions are wrong. No president—
even one as talented and well motivated as Obama—can get
a thing done in Washington unless the public is actively behind him. As FDR said in the reelection campaign of 1936
when a lady insisted that if she were to vote for him, he must
commit to a long list of objectives, "Ma'am, I want to do
those things, but you must make me."

If you believe Obama and the Democrats didn't push hard
enough in Obama's first four years to get done the things
you believe in, you and others have got to push harder. I'm
writing these words during the 2012 campaign, and don't
know if Obama will be reelected, or which party will control
the House or the Senate. Even if Obama is reelected and
the Democrats gain control of both chambers, you'll need
to become more active to give Obama and the Democrats
the political support they need to do what must be done in
Obama's second term. If he's not reelected, or if the Democrats lose control over both chambers, you'll need to become
even more active—not only to stop the regressives from

moving America backward but also to lay the groundwork for the next elections and beyond. You also need to organize *against* the regressives. Don't be fooled by the lies they're telling, and don't let others be fooled. The more you know and understand, the more powerful you will be at mobilizing others.

You can't accomplish much on your own. You have to join with others and pull in many more. Legislators don't pay much attention to complaints or demands from individual constituents (unless those constituents come armed with lots of campaign contributions), but they pay attention when those complaints or demands come from hundreds of constituents. The media likewise overlook press conferences organized by small groups, small demonstrations, and modest shows of political clout. But thousands of people gathered together can create news. And when tens of thousands turn out to vote for candidates who will support a progressive agenda, the media begin to see the makings of a political movement.

To achieve strength of numbers, you need to understand one of the basic rules of leadership: leadership doesn't necessitate formal authority. You don't need a fancy title in order to be a leader. I've known senators and cabinet officers and even presidents who never exercised much leadership; I've also met CEOs of large companies and the heads of vast foundations who failed to lead. Yet I've also known or met people with no formal authority who were extraordinary leaders—who mobilized, energized, and organized large numbers of people and thereby changed the direction of history. One of my favorites, Dolores Huerta, co-founded (with Cesar Chavez) the National Farm Workers Association, which later became the United Farm Workers. In 1966,

Huerta negotiated a contract between the farmworkers and the Schenley Wine Company; it was the first time farmworkers effectively negotiated a contract to improve their pay and working conditions. Or think of other great leaders who had no formal authority but changed the world—Martin Luther King Jr., Mahatma Gandhi, Nelson Mandela.

Leaders get people to actively work on what needs to be done. To do this, leaders need to help people overcome the four "work-avoidance mechanisms" that most of the rest of us carry around in our heads. Those mechanisms are *denial* that a problem exists, the desire to *escape* responsibility even when we recognize the problem, the tendency to *scapegoat* others for causing it, and—worst of all—*cynicism* about the possibility of ever remedying the problem. In order to mobilize, energize, and organize others to reverse the regressive drift of America and reclaim our economy and our democracy, you will need to convince many people of the truth that America is in imminent danger of becoming a plutocracy, even if they'd rather deny that reality. You'll need to show them that they can't escape from that truth: it's impossible for any of us or our families to have full and prosperous lives at the same time much of the rest of our population is becoming poorer and more economically insecure. You'll have to dissuade them from blaming immigrants, the poor, government workers, union workers, or even the rich for what is occurring, because such scapegoating merely divides us from one another and makes it more difficult to reverse this trend. And you must fight their cynicism and enable them to understand the situation *is* reversible: we have done it before and will do so again.

To exercise true leadership, you also need to get out of your ideological bubble. If most of the people you talk with agree

with you, you're wasting your time. You need to engage with people who may disagree or who haven't thought hard about the issues. Reach across to independents, even to Republicans and self-styled Tea Partiers. Find people who are willing to listen to the facts and are open to arguments and ideas, regardless of the label they apply to themselves. We need them.

Occasionally, I come across demonstrators who are holding signs on street corners where I live, in Berkeley, California. Sometimes the signs ask drivers to honk if they agree that America should cut its defense budget or raise taxes on the rich or that climate change must be reversed. As you can imagine, those street corners can become fairly noisy. I appreciate the effort these demonstrators are making, but I wish they'd do it in places where fewer drivers would honk, and engage those who disagree with them in discussion rather than merely hold up signs. It's too easy in modern America to preach to the converted, because it's increasingly easy to surround ourselves only with people who share our views.

Discussion isn't enough. You also need to express yourself in ways that enable those who may initially disagree with you to understand. Appeal to the moral values you and they share. Avoid violence. Violence can put you on the front page, but it will not capture the hearts and minds of those you need to convince. You'll be most convincing when you combine moral clarity with undeniable facts and common sense.

Look for organizing opportunities—teachable moments that illustrate why a policy currently in place is wrongheaded or why another approach is needed. For example, on the first Friday of every month the Labor Department reports the rate of unemployment, how many new jobs have been created, and what's happened to wages in the previous month. It should also be a day to look at corporate profits, CEO pay, and how many jobs American corporations have created abroad. That would help foster discussion and debate (and mobilizations and demonstrations if the trends continue to worsen) about what's happening to the real economy and what needs to be done to make it work for everyone instead of a very few. Tax days (April 15 when most taxes are due, as well as June 15, September 15, and January 15, when small businesses and contract workers have to pay estimated taxes) are occasions to point out that if the rich don't pay their fair share, the rest of us suffer from deteriorating public services or we have to make up the shortfall by paying more taxes. Be on the lookout for reports showing how much money is going into super PACs, what large corporations are spend-

ing to influence elected officials, which elected and appointed officials are taking jobs in lobbying firms or on Wall
Street—and make sure to share them widely.

Don't think you can be much of an activist by merely sitting behind your computer. I come across many good people who spend many hours online, disseminating petitions
or raising money for causes they believe in. I admire them
for it, but they need to bear in mind that the sheer conve-
nience of online political activism reduces its political po-
tency. Elected representatives who receive virtual petitions
know how little work they require relative to the exhausting
tasks of knocking on doors to get signatures or getting out
the vote. All too often, virtual organizations and movements
are fleeting. Their "members" feel no loyalty or connection
to one another. Direct contacts, on the other hand, are more
enduring. When people join together in person—when they
sacrifice evenings to meet up—they can build the trust and
energy required for the long haul. Those who say they don't
have time to meet aren't being truthful; if they have time
to watch hours of television or play on their laptops, they
can make the time to join with others for the future of their
communities and their nation.

Get out of your issue cocoon. Too often, progressives
become obsessed with one particular issue that becomes
"their" fight, to the exclusion of everything else. Don't get
me wrong. It's fine to fight for more efficient fuels or against
climate change, or both; good to be concerned about human
rights abuses or to push for gay rights or reproductive rights;
worthwhile to mobilize around the needs of children, a
single-payer health-care system, or cuts in military spending. But don't be so mesmerized by any single issue—and
don't allow others to become so single-minded about their

own fights—that we fail to join together on the bigger stuff that's making it harder for the voices of average Americans to be heard on all of these issues and others: the growing concentration of income, wealth, and political power at the top; the increasing clout of global corporations and Wall Street; and the corruption of our democracy.

Don't focus solely on Washington. Elections for president and Congress are obviously important, but in many respects the people elected to state and local offices have more day-to-day impact, making important decisions that affect the lives of countless people. Nor should you focus entirely on elections. Participate in corporate campaigns. Consumer boycotts of companies responsible for the largest political contributions, media attention to companies that award their top executives the fattest compensation packages while laying off the most workers, and pressure on their key investors can be important aspects of a broad-based campaign to end the rigged corporate game.

Perhaps the hardest thing of all is to be patient. I don't mean that you should be content or be willing to postpone what must be done. But you need to understand that altering the structure of power and widening opportunity require years of hard work, as those who toiled for the Civil Rights and Voting Rights Acts, or have been working for the rights of the disabled and gays, would tell you. It took thirty years of continuous fulmination for women to get the right to vote; fifty years of agitation before employers were required to bargain with unionized workers. Those who benefit from the prevailing allocation of power and wealth don't give up their privileged positions without a fight, and they usually have more resources at their disposal than the insurgents. Take satisfaction from small victories, but don't be discouraged or fall into cynicism, and don't let others do so, either. And don't allow yourself or others to burn out. I've known many activists who take a kind of masochistic delight in working themselves to exhaustion. Eventually, their health suffers or their emotional resilience disappears. They reach a breaking point and cannot go on. These people don't know how to pace themselves for the marathon run of a political movement.

Finally, instead of waiting for candidates to emerge with agendas and policy positions, take an active role in creating those agendas and get candidates to run on them. Tell incumbents you and others will work your hearts out to get them reelected on the condition they campaign on that agenda. Then, if and when they're elected, keep up the heat and the support.

Too many of us think political activism begins a few

months before Election Day and ends when winners are announced. I can't tell you how many political campaigns I've been involved with (even my own, briefly, for governor of Massachusetts) that demanded so much time and energy that there was none left once the results came in. That's a big mistake. The day after Election Day is the real beginning. That's when a loud and determined progressive movement needs to put pressure on newly elected officials and keep the pressure on. They must know that you and others like you will continue to mobilize support for a progressive agenda, reward them for pushing it, and hold them accountable in the next election cycle if they don't; that you will even go so far as to run candidates against them in their next primary—candidates who will run on that agenda.

The following are samples of what I mean. The first is an offer to people who hold public office, or who might want to hold office, to get behind them if they'll work toward a progressive agenda. It's meant not as a "litmus test"—not a strict or nonnegotiable set of demands—but as a practical guide to what we should expect our elected officials to do as a condition of receiving our support and benefiting from our hard work to get them elected. The second is a prototype of a different kind—a "corporate pledge of allegiance" around which progressives might organize to make large companies more accountable.

An Offer to Earn and Retain Our Support

We are prepared to work our hearts out for you to be elected and remain in office as long as you commit to the following agenda:

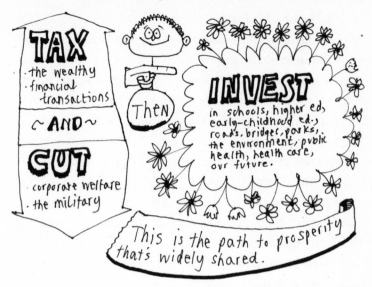

RAISE THE TAX RATE ON THE
RICH TO WHAT IT WAS BEFORE 1981

The top 1 percent has an almost unprecedented share of the nation's wealth and income yet the lowest tax rate in thirty years. Meanwhile, America faces colossal budget deficits that have already meant devastating cuts in education, infrastructure, and the safety nets we depend on.

The rich must pay at the same rate they did in the 1950s and 1960s. Income in excess of $1 million should be taxed at 70 percent. There should be more tax brackets at the top and higher rates in each of those top brackets. Absurdly, the top bracket is now set at $388,350 with a tax rate of 35 percent; the second-highest bracket, at 33 percent, starts at $178,650 for individuals. But the big money is way higher. And all sources of income, including capital gains, should be treated the same. It's scandalous that the four hundred richest Americans should pay an average of 17 percent tax on their incomes, a rate lower than that paid by many in the middle class. That's because so much of the income of the super-rich is considered capital gains, now taxed at only 15 percent. Close this loophole. (Don't penalize true entrepreneurs, though. If owners have held their assets for at least twenty years, keep their capital gains low.)

A 30 percent minimum tax on millionaires is a start, as is letting the 2001 and 2003 Bush tax cuts expire for taxpayers making over $250,000 a year, which would return the capital gains rate to 20 percent and the top rate on income and dividends to 39.6 percent. But that's just a start. It still falls short of what's needed to tame the nation's projected budget deficit and do everything else America must do. Sixty years ago Americans earning over $1 million in today's dollars paid 55.2 percent of it in income taxes, after taking all deductions and credits. If they were taxed at that rate now, they'd pay at least $80 billion more annually, which would reduce the budget deficit by about $1 trillion over the next ten years.

Put a 2 Percent Surtax on the Wealth of the Richest One-Half of 1 Percent

The richest one-half of 1 percent of Americans, each with over $7.2 million of assets, own 28 percent of the nation's total wealth. Given this almost unprecedented concentration, and considering what the nation needs to do to rebuild our schools and infrastructure, as well as tame the budget deficit, a surtax is warranted. It would generate another $70 billion a year, and $750 billion over the decade.

Put a One-Half of 1 Percent Tax
on All Financial Transactions

This would bring in more than $250 billion over ten years while slowing speculators and reducing the wild gyrations of financial markets.

The three changes above would add up to $2 trillion over ten years—a significant slice off the long-term budget deficit. Every one of these tax changes can be accomplished if Americans understand what's really at stake. If the rich don't pay their fair share of taxes, the rest of us will have to bear more of a burden. That burden will come in the form of either higher taxes on us or less money for the things we depend on—including health care, education, infrastructure, and national defense.

Cut the Military Budget More Than Scheduled

Without a new budget agreement, nearly $500 billion of automatic across-the-board cuts will be made in the defense budget over the next decade. But this isn't nearly enough. In the next five years, the Pentagon will still spend more than $2.7 trillion, closer to $3 trillion when adjusted for inflation.

Hundreds of billions more can be saved without jeopardizing the nation's security by ending weapons systems designed for an age of conventional warfare. For example, the F-35 fleet of stealth fighters, whose performance has been awful—the costliest Pentagon procurement project in history—should be jettisoned. Real arms control could save billions more. The number of deployed strategic nuclear weapons, ballistic missile submarines, and intercontinental ballistic missiles should be cut. The Navy and Air Force budgets should be reduced.

Most of the action is with the Army, Marines, and Special Forces. Billions more can be saved by eliminating programs no one can justify and few can understand.

Use Medicare to Control Soaring Health-Care Costs

An independent commission to come up with cuts in Medicare if its yearly costs rise half a percent faster than the national economy is better than the Republican plan for turning Medicare into vouchers whose value won't rise as fast as health-care costs. But it still assumes that the rising Medicare costs are the fundamental problem. The real problem is a wildly inefficient health-care system—for which Medicare can be the solution. Some features of the new health-care law will slow the rise of costs—insurance exchanges, for example, could give consumers clearer comparative information about what they're getting for their insurance payments—but the law doesn't go nearly far enough.

Medicare's huge bargaining leverage over drug companies and health-care providers should be used to bring down health-care costs and to move from a pay-for-service system to a *pay-for-healthy-outcomes* system. We're spending almost two and a half times more on health care per person than any other advanced nation, yet the typical American doesn't live as long as the citizens of those nations and we have a higher rate of infant mortality. That's because here doctors and hospitals have every incentive to spend on unnecessary tests, drugs, and procedures but little incentive to keep people healthy.

For example, almost 95 percent of cases of lower-back pain are best relieved through physical therapy. But American doctors and hospitals routinely do expensive MRIs and then refer patients to orthopedic surgeons who often do even more costly surgery—because there's not much money in physical therapy. Twenty percent of the people who go into a hospital for diabetes, asthma, or a heart condition are back within a month; they'd do better if a nurse visited them at home—a common practice in other advanced countries—to answer their questions and make sure they are taking their medications. But nurses don't make home visits to Americans with acute conditions, because hospitals and nurses aren't paid for making them. Instead of reimbursing doctors and hospitals for the costly tests, drugs, and procedures, pay them for keeping people healthy.

Fight for Medicare for All

The Republicans' plan would simply funnel money into the hands of for-profit insurers whose administrative costs are far higher than Medicare's. The real answer to providing broad coverage and keeping a lid on costs is to allow anyone at any age to join Medicare.

Medicare's administrative costs are in the range of 3 percent—well below the 5–10 percent costs borne by large companies that self-insure, even further below the administrative costs of companies in the small-group market (amounting to 25–27 percent of premiums), and much lower than the administrative costs of individual insurance (30 percent). It's even below the 11 percent costs of private plans under Medicare Advantage, the current private insurance option under Medicare. Medicare for all would reduce the colossal waste in the current system. Right now we're spending $30 billion a year fixing medical errors—the worst rate among advanced countries—partly because we keep patient records on computers that can't share the data. Patient records are continually rewritten on pieces of paper and then reentered into different computers, which leads to errors. Meanwhile, administrative costs are eating up 15–30 percent of all health-care spending in the United States. That's twice the rate of most other advanced nations. This money goes mainly into collecting money: doctors collect from hospitals and insurers, hospitals collect from insurers, insurers collect from companies or from policyholders. At some hospitals, billing clerks outnumber physicians. A third of nursing hours are devoted to documenting tests and procedures so insurers have proof.

Estimates of how much would be saved by extending Medicare to cover the entire population range from $58 billion to $400 billion a year. More Americans would get quality health care, and the long-term budget crisis would be sharply reduced.

The new health-care law requires people to buy health insurance from private insurers. This "individual mandate" spreads the risk of someone needing medical care to younger or healthier people, thereby enabling private insurers to afford to take on older or sicker customers with preexisting medical conditions or to maintain coverage indefinitely for people who become seriously ill. Yet the individual mandate is deeply unpopular. It not only offends libertarian sensibilities but also worries some moderates and liberals who fear private insurers will charge too much because of insufficient competition in the industry. Republicans see an opportunity here to destroy the new health-care law by attacking the individual mandate.

But there's another way to spread medical risks across the public. It's the same framework used by Social Security and Medicare—public insurance financed by payroll taxes. Not only are these programs enormously popular—"Don't take

away my Medicare!" was a rallying cry among some conservative populists during the debates over the health-care
law—but they rest on a more widely accepted relationship
among the individual, the government, and the market. Both
Medicare and Social Security require every working American to "buy" them, but the purchase happens automatically
in the form of a deduction from everyone's paycheck. Such
payments are viewed not as federal mandates that encroach
upon individual freedoms, or as payoffs to private companies
likely to make even more money from mandatory purchases
of their products, but as well-deserved entitlements. Americans are accustomed to paying for public insurance through
their payroll taxes. Indeed, the biggest problem with Social
Security and Medicare is they're so popular that politicians
have had a hard time trimming their benefits to match payroll
tax revenues.

Republican attacks on the individual mandate will create an opportunity for policy jujitsu. We should amend the
new health-care law and create Medicare for all—premised
on payroll taxes and public insurance, the system Americans
prefer. The public will be behind it, as will the courts.

Use These Added Revenues and Budget Savings to Invest in Public Goods— Especially Education and Infrastructure

The state of the nation's schools in poor and middle-class
communities is a scandal that makes a mockery of the ideal
of equal opportunity, further widens inequality, and under-
mines the competitiveness of the economy. Most teachers in
these schools are paid less than $50,000 a year, and class-
rooms are crammed. These schools can't afford textbooks or
science labs, and they've abandoned after-school programs

and courses like history and art. The reason: School budgets across America depend substantially on local property taxes that continue to drop in lower-income communities. The federal government should come to their rescue. States also need help financing early childhood education so that every preschooler can begin school ready to learn. And the federal government should help restore the nation's system of public higher education, which has been decimated by state budget cuts.

Meanwhile, America's infrastructure is crumbling. Our roads, bridges, water and sewer systems, subways and other forms of public transit, gas pipelines, ports, airports, and school buildings are all in desperate need of repair. Deferred maintenance is taking a huge toll. The American Society of Civil Engineers has given the nation's infrastructure an overall grade of D. The percentage of the national economy going to infrastructure continues to drop—from 1 percent in 1960 to barely three-tenths of 1 percent in 2012. It's time to rebuild America while at the same time expanding high-speed Internet and modernizing the electricity grid.

Over the long term the only way to improve the living standards of most Americans is to invest in our people—especially their educations, and the communications and transportation systems linking them together and with the rest of the world. Spending on these is fundamentally different from other categories of government spending because these outlays are investments in the future productivity of our people. There's no problem with borrowing in order to finance investments in the future. Families do it all the time. While it might be irresponsible for a family to go into debt in order to finance a worldwide cruise, it would be highly responsible for the same family to borrow money in order to help finance their kids' college educations. Businesses also borrow in order to increase future productivity. If they didn't, they'd be out of business. Such borrowing makes sense as long as the return on the investment is higher than the cost (principal plus interest) of the borrowing.

It's cheaper than ever for the United States to borrow. In 2012 the yield on the ten-year Treasury bill was hovering around 2 percent. That's because global investors sought the safety of dollars. Europe was in a debt crisis, many developing nations were gripped by fears the contagion would spread to them, the Japanese economy remained in poor condition, and China's growth was slowing. These conditions won't continue forever, of course, but the dollar will remain a safe haven for many years. It's the ideal time to redevelop the public goods America desperately needs.

RESURRECT THE GLASS-STEAGALL ACT

There is no good reason that banks should ever be permitted to use people's bank deposits, insured by the federal government, to place risky bets on the banks' own behalf. Yet Wall Street lobbyists have made sure the new Dodd-Frank law has enough loopholes to allow financiers to continue to gamble with other people's money. The so-called Volcker Rule in the new Dodd-Frank Act was designed as a compromise—a kind of Glass-Steagall lite—but under the pressure of Wall Street's lobbyists it is too weak to do the job. The giant bets JPMorgan placed on risky derivatives that went bad in the spring of 2012 should serve as a loud warning. One way to stop the looting—or at the least limit the ability of Wall Street's biggest banks to make unreasonably risky bets—is to bring back Glass-Steagall. The act was put in place after the crash of 1929 to prevent financiers from gambling with people's bank deposits but was repealed in 1999, and its repeal contributed to the crash of 2008.

CAP THE SIZE OF WALL STREET'S BIGGEST BANKS

The other sad lesson of the Dodd-Frank legislation is that Wall Street is too powerful to allow effective regulation of it. We should have learned that lesson in 2008 as the Street brought the rest of the economy—and much of the world— to its knees. The Street's leviathans do not generate benefits to society proportional to their size and influence. To the contrary, they represent a clear and present danger to our economy and our democracy. The best way to avoid another bailout is to break them up and then put a cap on the maximum size of the biggest banks.

There is precedent. The Sherman Antitrust Act of 1890 and its companion, the Clayton Act of 1914, were designed not only to improve economic efficiency by reducing the market power of economic giants like the railroads and oil companies but also to prevent companies from becoming so large that their political power would undermine democracy. Trustbusters during the first decades of the twentieth century tamed American industry and arguably saved capitalism from its own excesses. We've come to a similar juncture a century later, but this time it's big finance that has to be tamed.

In April 2012, the Dallas branch of the Federal Reserve Bank came to the same conclusion, recommending that the biggest banks be broken up and their size be capped. This is particularly notable in that the Dallas Fed is one of the most conservative of all Fed branches. But it knows from experience. Texas was ground zero in the savings and loan crisis that ripped through America in the 1980s, imposing huge losses on the state.

The Wall Street banks were too big to fail before the bailout and are even bigger now. Twenty years ago, the ten largest banks on the Street held 10 percent of America's total bank assets. Now the six largest hold over 70 percent. And the biggest four have a larger market share than ever. Their size gives them special privileges at the Fed—lower interest rate charges and special drawing rights—that provide them with a competitive advantage over their smaller rivals. And with this advantage they're sure to grow even larger. They must be broken up.

Require Big Banks to Modify Underwater Mortgages

In February 2012, five big banks reached a deal with government authorities over dubious mortgage practices and foreclosure abuses. In exchange for reducing the principal on the mortgage loans of distressed homeowners by $17 billion, the banks were absolved of many legal claims against them. But given that close to eleven million borrowers were underwater on their loans by about $700 billion, this settlement was barely a drop in a huge bucket. Although some homeowners should have known they were borrowing excessively, most reasonably assumed housing prices would continue to rise. It wasn't their fault that the banks created a housing bubble that burst, causing home values to plummet. And most of the banks' wrongdoing has never been fully investigated, including possible tax, trust, and securities violations.

There must be a new investigation into mortgage abuses, a broader inquiry that could lead to a much larger package of relief. Allowing millions of homeowners to remain in their homes and reversing the collapse of housing prices would be good for almost everyone, including banks whose balance sheets have been weakened by the slide in home values.

Meanwhile, the bankruptcy laws should be changed to allow struggling homeowners to declare bankruptcy on their primary residence. This will give homeowners more bargaining leverage with the banks to reorganize their mortgage loans. Why should the owners of commercial property and second homes be allowed to include these assets in bankruptcy but not regular homeowners?

GET BIG MONEY OUT OF POLITICS

Finally, in order to get any of this—and more—done, we need to get big money out of politics. If income and wealth in America were as widely shared as in the first three decades after World War II, we'd have less reason to worry about money in politics. But with an almost unprecedented concentration of wealth at the very top, unbridled money in politics poses a clear and present danger to our democracy. The Supreme Court's 2010 decision in *Citizens United v. Federal Election Commission* invites the worst corruption we have witnessed since the Gilded Age.

We must clean up the mess the Supreme Court has created. We need Supreme Court justices who will reverse the ruling in *Citizens United*. And a constitutional amendment making clear that corporations are not citizens entitled to contribute to political elections and that Congress has the power to set limits on campaign spending.

In the meantime, there must be full public disclosure of all donors to super PACs and other organizations that engage in political advertising. Corporations should have to get the approval of shareholders before spending corporate funds—the shareholders' money—on politics. A shareholder who doesn't approve should be refunded for such expenses in proportion to his or her share of the company.

Finally, we must have a system of public financing available to any presidential or congressional candidate supported by at least 5 percent of the voting public. These funds would provide $2 for every $1 raised from small donors (each giving no more than $1,000) so candidates can succeed without relying on a few billionaires pumping unlimited sums into super PACs.

One step can be taken without congressional approval: an executive order forcing big government contractors to disclose their political spending, and banning all political activity by companies receiving more than half their revenues from the U.S. government. Lockheed Martin, the nation's largest contractor, got more than $19 billion in federal contracts in 2011 while spending millions lobbying Congress to get even more. Sixty-four of Lockheed's lobbyists were former congressional staffers, Pentagon officials, or White House aides. Two were former members of Congress. Lockheed has also been spending more than $3 million a year on political contributions to friendly members of Congress.

Lockheed is not alone. The ten biggest government contractors are all defense contractors. Every one of them gets most of its revenues from the federal government and uses a portion of that money to lobby for even more defense contracts.

That's one reason the defense procurement budget keeps growing. The drawdown of troops from Iraq in 2011 was supposed to save money, but Lockheed and other giant defense contractors have tried to funnel the anticipated savings into new weapons systems. In 2012, Lockheed delivered a budget bombshell with a proposed tab of more than $1 trillion for a fleet of F-35 Joint Strike Fighter jets. In the wake of the *Citizens United* ruling, there's no limit on what Lockheed and other defense contractors can spend on politics. That's why it's necessary to put an end to this increasingly expensive conflict of interest by banning all political activities by corporations getting more than half their revenues from the federal government.

So here's the deal: We'll give you a mandate to do all this and more, we'll work like hell to elect you or to make sure you're reelected, and we'll stand behind you as you try to get this agenda enacted. As long as you stand behind us and make this agenda your own.

THE CORPORATE PLEDGE OF ALLEGIANCE

If the Supreme Court and most regressives insist big American corporations are people that deserve to be treated as American citizens, and be given tax breaks and special advantages to create jobs here, we should expect those corporations to show some loyalty to this country. So why not have big American corporations take a pledge of allegiance to the United States? It wouldn't be a legal requirement. It would be entirely voluntary. Corporations that take the pledge would be able to say in their advertisements, "We pledge allegiance to the United States." And American consumers would be free to boycott those that don't take

HOW TO GET BiG MONEY OUT of POLiTiCS

① Reverse "Citizen's United"

CONSTITUTIONAL AMENDMENT
Money is not speech. Corporations are not people.

② Full disclosure

of who pays for all ads for or against any candidate.

③ Public financing:

VOTE FOR U.S.

match public dollars to any small donations, so candidates can't gain advantage by getting huge donations from fat cats, corporations, & Wall Street

the pledge. In fact, you might consider organizing just such a boycott.

Here's what a corporate pledge of allegiance might look like:

OUR CORPORATION PLEDGES ALLEGIANCE TO THE UNITED STATES OF AMERICA.

We pledge to create more jobs in the United States than we create outside the United States, either directly or in our foreign subsidiaries and subcontractors.

We further pledge that no more than 20 percent of our total labor costs will be outsourced abroad. If we have to lay off American workers at a time when we're profitable, we will give those workers severance payments equal to their weekly wage times the number of months they've worked for us.

We pledge to keep a lid on executive pay so no executive is paid more than fifty times the median pay of American workers. We define "pay" to include salary, bonuses, health benefits, pension benefits, deferred salary, stock options, and every other form of compensation.

We pledge to pay at least 30 percent of money earned in the United States in taxes to the United States. We won't shift our money to offshore tax havens, and we won't use accounting gimmicks to fake how much we earn.

We pledge not to use our money to influence elections.

This isn't too much to ask, is it? Again, it wouldn't be a legal requirement; corporations would be free to pledge or not to pledge. And consumers would be free to boycott those corporations that don't make the pledge or that disregard it.

But at least we'll know which corporations that enjoy the benefits of American citizenship act like American citizens. That's important this election year and beyond.

PRACTICING ACTIVE CITIZENSHIP

Not long ago I had a discussion with Jon Stewart, the wily impresario of Comedy Central's *Daily Show*. It was before a young audience who whooped and hollered at Stewart's antics and my hapless responses to them, but the topic we were debating was dead serious. I argued that the real reason Washington was letting so many of us down was so few of us were actively pushing our public officials to do the right thing. He said we elected them so we wouldn't have to be actively engaged in politics; that was their job. I said he was wrong: Citizenship entails more than voting on election days. Real citizenship requires ongoing engagement: knowing what needs to be done, getting the facts, and understanding the arguments, and then making enough of a ruckus—and organizing and mobilizing others to join you—so that what needs to be done gets done.

Most of us don't practice active citizenship, because we tell ourselves we're too busy for it. Yet we find time to do other things—swimming or crossword puzzles or playing cards or cooking. Maybe we make religion our focus, or golf. Or we devote ourselves to trying to make money in the stock market. The truth is we have the time. The real reason most of us don't practice citizenship is we don't know how. And we don't think it will do any good anyway.

I hope I've convinced you that you must at least try. You don't need to practice it full-time. It need not and should not become an obsession. But few things we possess and will hand on to our children and grandchildren are more precious than our democracy. And few things we believe in will affect the lives of our children and grandchildren more fundamentally than our commitment to equal opportunity and to a fair and just society. That precious possession and that fundamental ideal are both gravely endangered. They can be protected only by engaged citizens who know the truth and are willing to fight to reclaim our democracy and our economy.

How to begin? Here and now. You've already just about finished this book, which should help you connect the dots and understand what's happening, why the regressives are dangerously wrong, and what must be done. Share the book with your friends. Invite them over to talk about it. Ask if they'd be willing to join you in developing an "action agenda" for achieving progressive change in your community, or even at the state or national level. Bring others into the circle who might feel similarly and be helpful. Assign someone the task of finding other groups or organizations in your area aiming to do something similar, and reach out to them as well.

This is how progressive change occurs. This is how it has always occurred.

A FINAL NOTE ON THE BASIC CHOICE: REGRESSION OR PROGRESSION, SOCIAL DARWINISM OR THE PUBLIC GOOD

America is not the only place struggling with a collision between regressive forces lurching backward toward more authoritarian, intolerant, and unequal societies and progressive forces striving for more democracy, tolerance, and equal opportunity. The details differ, but the larger forces are similar. You see it in Europe, where many people are being squeezed by bankers insisting on austerity. You see it in Chile and Israel, where young people are revolting against limited opportunity and widening inequality. It's on view in the Middle East, where the "Arab spring" has turned into ongoing struggles to create functioning democracies. You see it even in China, where young and hourly workers are demanding more and where the surge toward inequality in recent years has been as breathtaking as the surge toward modern capitalism.

But it is likely to be in America—still the world's largest economy and its most influential practitioner of democracy— where the collision is most consequential. And I believe we will once again show the world that when our ideals are tested, we do not bend. We do not move backward. We do not tolerate rigged games.

The great arc of American history reveals an unmistakable pattern. Whenever privilege and power conspire to pull us backward, we eventually rally and move forward. Sometimes it takes an economic shock like the bursting of a giant speculative bubble; sometimes we just reach a tipping point where the frustrations of average Americans turn into action. Look at the progressive reforms between 1900 and 1916; the New Deal of the 1930s; the civil rights struggle of the 1950s and 1960s; the widening opportunities for women, minorities, people with disabilities, and gays, starting in the 1960s and continuing, in fits and starts, to the present day; and the environmental reforms of the 1970s. In each of these eras, regressive forces reignited the progressive ideals on which America is built. The result was fundamental reform.

It will happen again, but it will not happen automatically.

The nation's forward movement has always depended on the active engagement and commitment of vast numbers of Americans who were morally outraged by how far our economy and our democracy have strayed from our ideals and who committed to move beyond outrage to real reform.

Your outrage and your commitment are needed once again.

WE The People

— Getting Beyond Outrage —

Appendix

I believe President Obama's speech in Osawatomie—where Teddy Roosevelt gave his "New Nationalism" speech in 1910—will be remembered as the most important economic speech of his or any modern presidency in terms of connecting the dots, laying out the reasons behind our economic and political crises, and asserting a willingness to take on the powerful and the privileged who have gamed the system to their advantage. It's so important that I've included most of it here (along with, if you'll pardon me, my annotations):

> For most Americans, the basic bargain that made this country great has eroded. Long before the recession hit, hard work stopped paying off for too many people. Fewer and fewer of the folks who contributed to the success of our economy actu-

ally benefited from that success. Those at the very top grew
wealthier from their incomes and investments than ever be-
fore. But everyone else struggled with costs that were growing
and paychecks that weren't—and too many families found
themselves racking up more and more debt just to keep up.

He's absolutely right, and it's the first time he or any other
president clearly stated the long-term structural problem
that's been widening the gap between the very top and everyone else for thirty years—the breaking of the basic bargain linking pay to productivity gains.

For many years, credit cards and home equity loans papered
over the harsh realities of this new economy. But in 2008, the
house of cards collapsed.

Exactly. But the first papering over was when large numbers of women went into paid work, starting in the late
1970s and the 1980s, in order to prop up family incomes
that were stagnating or dropping because male wages were
under siege—from globalization, technological change, and
the decline of unions. Only when this coping mechanism
was exhausted, and when housing prices started to climb,
did Americans shift to credit cards and home equity loans as
a means of papering over the new harsh reality of an economy that was working for a minority at the top but not for
most of the middle class.

We all know the story by now: Mortgages sold to peo-
ple who couldn't afford them, or sometimes even understand
them. Banks and investors allowed to keep packaging the risk
and selling it off. Huge bets—and huge bonuses—made with

other people's money on the line. Regulators who were sup-
posed to warn us about the dangers of all this, but looked the
other way or didn't have the authority to look at all.

It was wrong. It combined the breathtaking greed of a few
with irresponsibility across the system. And it plunged our
economy and the world into a crisis from which we are still
fighting to recover. It claimed the jobs, homes, and the basic
security of millions—innocent, hardworking Americans who
had met their responsibilities but were still left holding the bag.

Precisely—and it was about time he used the term
"wrong" to describe Wall Street's antics and the abject failure of regulators (led by Alan Greenspan and the Fed) to
stop what was going on. These were among the remarks that
earned Obama the enmity of much of Wall Street—and en-
couraged them to empty their wallets for the Republicans in
2012. Nonetheless, these "wrongs" were only the proximate
cause of the economic crisis that befell the nation in 2008
and lingered for years after. The underlying cause was, as the
president said before, the breaking of the basic bargain linking pay to productivity.

Ever since, there has been a raging debate over the best
way to restore growth and prosperity, balance and fairness.
Throughout the country, it has sparked protests and political
movements—from the Tea Party to the people who have been
occupying the streets of New York and other cities. It's left
Washington in a near-constant state of gridlock. And it's been
the topic of heated and sometimes colorful discussion among
the men and women who are running for president.

But this isn't just another political debate. This is the
defining issue of our time. This is a make-or-break moment

> *for the middle class and all those who are fighting to get into*
> *the middle class. At stake is whether this will be a country*
> *where working people can earn enough to raise a family, build*
> *a modest savings, own a home, and secure their retirement.*

Right again. It is the defining issue of our time. But I wish he didn't lump the Tea Party in with the Occupiers. The former hates government; the latter focuses blame on Wall Street and corporate greed, just where the president did a moment ago.

> *Now, in the midst of this debate, there are some who seem to*
> *be suffering from a kind of collective amnesia. After all that's*
> *happened, after the worst economic crisis since the Great De-*
> *pression, they want to return to the same practices that got us*
> *into this mess. In fact, they want to go back to the same poli-*
> *cies that have stacked the deck against middle-class Americans*
> *for too many years. Their philosophy is simple: we are better*
> *off when everyone is left to fend for themselves and play by*
> *their own rules.*

He might have been a bit stronger here. The "they" who are suffering collective amnesia include many of the privileged and the powerful who have gained enormous wealth by using their political muscle to entrench their privilege and power. In other words, it's not simply or even mainly amnesia. It's a clear and concerted strategy, and it continues to pay off for them while imposing significant risk on the rest of the economy.

> *Well, I'm here to say they are wrong. I'm here to reaffirm my*
> *deep conviction that we are greater together than we are on*

our own. I believe that this country succeeds when everyone gets a fair shot, when everyone does their fair share, and when everyone plays by the same rules. Those aren't Democratic or Republican values; 1 percent values or 99 percent values. They're American values, and we have to reclaim them.

Amen.

> *... In 1910, Teddy Roosevelt came here, to Osawatomie, and laid out his vision for what he called a New Nationalism. "Our country," he said, ". . . means nothing unless it means the triumph of a real democracy . . . of an economic system under which each man shall be guaranteed the opportunity to show the best that there is in him."*

Some background: In 1909, Herbert Croly, a young political philosopher and journalist, argued in his best-selling book *The Promise of American Life* that the large American corporation should be regulated by the nation and directed toward national goals. "The constructive idea behind a policy of the recognition of semi-monopolistic corporations is, of course, the idea that they can be converted into economic agents . . . for the national economic interest," Croly wrote. Teddy Roosevelt's New Nationalism embraced Croly's idea.

> *For this, Roosevelt was called a radical, a socialist, even a communist. But today, we are a richer nation and a stronger democracy because of what he fought for in his last campaign: an eight-hour workday and a minimum wage for women; insurance for the unemployed, the elderly, and those with disabilities; political reform and a progressive income tax.*
>
> *Today, over one hundred years later, our economy has*

gone through another transformation. Over the last few decades, huge advances in technology have allowed businesses to do more with less, and made it easier for them to set up shop and hire workers anywhere in the world. And many of you know firsthand the painful disruptions this has caused for a lot of Americans.

Factories where people thought they would retire suddenly picked up and went overseas, where the workers were cheaper. Steel mills that needed a thousand employees are now able to do the same work with a hundred, so that layoffs were too often permanent, not just a temporary part of the business cycle. These changes didn't just affect blue-collar workers. If you were a bank teller or a phone operator or a travel agent, you saw many in your profession replaced by ATMs or the Internet. Today, even higher-skilled jobs like accountants and middle management can be outsourced to countries like China and India. And if you're someone whose job can be done cheaper by a computer or someone in another country, you don't have a lot of leverage with your employer when it comes to asking for better wages and benefits—especially since fewer Americans today are part of a union.

Now, just as there was in Teddy Roosevelt's time, there's been a certain crowd in Washington for the last few decades who respond to this economic challenge with the same old tune. "The market will take care of everything," they tell us. If only we cut more regulations and cut more taxes—especially for the wealthy—our economy will grow stronger. Sure, there will be winners and losers. But if the winners do really well, jobs and prosperity will eventually trickle down to everyone else. And even if prosperity doesn't trickle down, they argue, that's the price of liberty.

It's a simple theory—one that speaks to our rugged indi-
vidualism and healthy skepticism of too much government. It
fits well on a bumper sticker. Here's the problem: It doesn't
work. It's never worked. It didn't work when it was tried in
the decade before the Great Depression. It's not what led to
the incredible postwar boom of the '50s and '60s. And it didn't
work when we tried it during the last decade.

The president is advocating Croly's proposal that large
corporations be regulated for the nation's good. But he's up-
dating Croly. The next paragraphs are important:

Remember that in those years, in 2001 and 2003, Congress
passed two of the most expensive tax cuts for the wealthy in
history, and what did they get us? The slowest job growth in
half a century. Massive deficits that have made it much harder
to pay for the investments that built this country and provided
the basic security that helped millions of Americans reach and
stay in the middle class—things like education and infrastruc-
ture; science and technology; Medicare and Social Security.

Remember that in those years, thanks to some of the folks
who are running Congress now, we had weak regulation and
little oversight, and what did that get us? Insurance compa-
nies that jacked up people's premiums with impunity, and
denied care to the patients who were sick. Mortgage lenders
that tricked families into buying homes they couldn't afford. A
financial sector where irresponsibility and lack of basic over-
sight nearly destroyed our entire economy.

We simply cannot return to this brand of you're on your
own economics if we're serious about rebuilding the middle
class in this country. We know that it doesn't result in a strong

economy. It results in an economy that invests too little in its people and its future. It doesn't result in a prosperity that trickles down. It results in a prosperity that's enjoyed by fewer and fewer of our citizens.

Look at the statistics. In the last few decades, the average income of the top 1 percent has gone up by more than 250 percent, to $1.2 million per year. For the top one hundredth of 1 percent, the average income is now $27 million per year. The typical CEO who used to earn about 30 times more than his or her workers now earns 110 times more. And yet, over the last decade, the incomes of most Americans have actually fallen by about 6 percent.

This is the first time the president—any president—has publicly and unequivocally emphasized this grotesque trend. Now see how he connects this with the deterioration of our economy and our democracy:

This kind of inequality—a level we haven't seen since the Great Depression—hurts us all. When middle-class families can no longer afford to buy the goods and services that businesses are selling, it drags down the entire economy, from top to bottom. America was built on the idea of broad-based prosperity—that's why a CEO like Henry Ford made it his mission to pay his workers enough so that they could buy the cars they made. It's also why a recent study showed that countries with less inequality tend to have stronger and steadier economic growth over the long run.

Inequality also distorts our democracy. It gives an outsized voice to the few who can afford high-priced lobbyists and un-limited campaign contributions, and runs the risk of selling

out our democracy to the highest bidder. And it leaves everyone else rightly suspicious that the system in Washington is
rigged against them—that our elected representatives aren't
looking out for the interests of most Americans.

More fundamentally, this kind of gaping inequality gives
lie to the promise at the very heart of America: that this is the
place where you can make it if you try. We tell people that in
this country, even if you're born with nothing, hard work can
get you into the middle class; and that your children will have
the chance to do even better than you. That's why immigrants
from around the world flocked to our shores.

And now he shows what massive inequality has done to
equal opportunity and how it has eroded upward mobility:

And yet, over the last few decades, the rungs on the ladder
of opportunity have grown farther and farther apart, and the
middle class has shrunk. A few years after World War II, a
child who was born into poverty had a slightly better than
fifty-fifty chance of becoming middle-class as an adult. By
1980, that chance fell to around 40 percent. And if the trend
of rising inequality over the last few decades continues, it's estimated that a child born today will only have a one-in-three
chance of making it to the middle class.

It's heartbreaking enough that there are millions of working families in this country who are now forced to take their
children to food banks for a decent meal. But the idea that
those children might not have a chance to climb out of that
situation and back into the middle class, no matter how hard
they work? That's inexcusable. It's wrong. It flies in the face
of everything we stand for.

What should we do about this? We should not turn to protectionism or become neo-Luddites, nor should we turn to some version of government planning:

> *Fortunately, that's not a future we have to accept. Because there's another view about how we build a strong middle class in this country—a view that's truer to our history; a vision that's been embraced by people of both parties for more than two hundred years. It's not a view that we should somehow turn back technology or put up walls around America. It's not a view that says we should punish profit or success or pretend that government knows how to fix all society's problems. It's a view that says in America, we are greater together—when everyone engages in fair play, everyone gets a fair shot, everyone does their fair share.*
>
> *So what does that mean for restoring middle-class security in today's economy?*
>
> *It starts by making sure that everyone in America gets a fair shot at success. The truth is, we'll never be able to compete with other countries when it comes to who's best at letting their businesses pay the lowest wages or pollute as much as they want. That's a race to the bottom that we can't win—and shouldn't want to win. Those countries don't have a strong middle class. They don't have our standard of living.*
>
> *. . . The fact is, this crisis has left a deficit of trust between Main Street and Wall Street. And major banks that were rescued by the taxpayers have an obligation to go the extra mile in helping to close that deficit. At minimum, they should be remedying past mortgage abuses that led to the financial crisis, and working to keep responsible homeowners in their home. We're going to keep pushing them to provide more time for*

unemployed homeowners to look for work without having to worry about immediately losing their house.

I wish the Obama administration had made this a condition for the banks receiving bailouts. Nonetheless, on December 6, 2011, President Obama correctly diagnosed the challenge facing America—and laid out the argument for increasing taxes on the rich, investing in the rest of us, requiring corporations and Wall Street banks that reap benefits from being in America to create good jobs for Americans, and protecting our democracy from being corrupted by money. Here, finally, was the Barack Obama many of us thought we had elected in 2008.

One hopes this message will be taken to heart by Americans, and that those whom we elect to the highest offices in the land will reverse the growing inequities and game-rigging practices now undermining the American economy and American democracy.

But they cannot and will not do this on their own. We must make them.

Acknowledgments

My abiding appreciation once again goes to my assistant, Rebecca Boles, for her steadfast and cheerful help in preparing this book for publication, and to Manuel Castrillo, for his superb technical support. As with my other books, this one would not have happened but for the thoughtful guidance of my longtime editor and friend, Jon Segal, and the sage advice of my literary agent, Rafe Sagalyn. I'm also grateful to Jeff Alexander for helping guide this into paperback. I owe special thanks to my students and colleagues at the University of California, Berkeley, whose interest in and commitment to a better world are boundless.

REASON
Why Liberals Will Win the Battle for America

In the pages of *Reason*, Reich mounts a defense of classic liberalism that's also a guide for rolling back twenty years of radical conservative domination of our politics and political culture. Reich shows how liberals can shift the focus of the values debate from behavior in the bedroom to malfeasance in the boardroom, and reclaim patriotism from those who equate it with preemptive war-making and the suppression of dissent.

Politics

THE RESURGENT LIBERAL
And Other Unfashionable Prophecies

In *The Resurgent Liberal*, one of the most tough-minded bearers of the torch of liberalism not only champions a cause but looks fairly and unblinkingly at the opposition. Robert B. Reich carefully examines the four "parables" conservatives have exploited to monopolize American politics and outlines what liberals must do to take it back.

Political Science

SUPERCAPITALISM
The Transformation of Business, Democracy, and Everyday Life

From one of America's foremost economic and political thinkers comes a vital analysis of our new hypercompetitive and turbocharged global economy and the effect it is having on American democracy. With his customary wit and insight, Reich shows how widening inequality of income and wealth, heightened job insecurity, and corporate corruption are merely the logical results of a system in which politicians are more beholden to the influence of business lobbyists than to the voters who elected them.

Politics

There is no longer such a thing as an American economy, says Robert B. Reich. What does it mean to be a nation when money, goods, and services know no borders? And how can our country best ensure that *all* citizens have a share in the new global economy? Reich defines the real challenge facing the United States in this trailblazing book. Original, readable, and vastly informed, *The Work of Nations* is certain to set the standard for the next generation of policy-makers.

Economics

VINTAGE BOOKS
Available wherever books are sold.
www.randomhouse.com